Hetty on Hold

Hetty on Hold

by
Martha Sears West

CLEAN KIND WORLD
Los Angeles

CLEAN KIND WORLD
Los Angeles

Text and Illustrations Copyright © 2020, 2019 by Martha Sears West.
Edited by Page Mallett

Hetty on Hold
Fifth in Series

All rights reserved.
This publication may not be reproduced or transmitted in any form or by any means, without permission from the author/illustrator or publisher.

Young Adult/Bildungsroman: This novel is a work of fiction. Names, characters, places, and incidents are either products of the author's imagination or are used fictitiously. All characters are fictional, and any similarity to people living or dead, events, or locales is purely coincidental.

Library of Congress Preassigned Control Number 2017958478.
Print ISBN 978-1-7329799-4-9
Audio 978-1-7329799-2-5
eBook 978-0-9908693-7-5

The story begins in 1964.

CleanKindWorldBooks.com   ParkPlacePress.com
Toll Free 800·616·8081 · Fax 323·953·9850 · Shipping 435·764·4545
2016 Cummings · Los Angeles CA 90027
ymaddox@CleanKindWorldBooks.com

Martha Sears West titles are available online and in fine bookstores:
· *Jake, Dad and the Worm* · *Longer Than Forevermore* ·
· *Rhymes and Doodles from a Wind-up Toy* ·

· *Hetty* · *Hetty Happens* · *Hetty or Not* · *Honeymoon Summer* · *Hetty on Hold* ·
are available in print, audio, and eBook.

10 9 8 6 5 4 3 2 1
Printed in the United States of America

Steve,
thank you
for the adventure.
I miss your counsel, love, and encouragement.

With Page's continued guidance,
Hetty came to life.

CONTENTS

CHAPTER ONE..1
    Intertwined
    Rice
    The Phone Call
    In Recovery
    The Letter
    Keeping Score
    Family Conference

CHAPTER TWO..27
    Sweet Victory
    The Dream
    Whoopty-do
    You Watermelon
    The Understanding
    Freydis Returns
    Hamlet to the Rescue
    To the Cemetery

CHAPTER THREE..53
    Nobody Will Know
    Torn
    A Stunning Day
    Protecting LuvCon
    Nuts
    Squeezing Out the Answer
    The Outing
    Not Squishy
    Cold Stone Steps

CHAPTER FOUR...79
    Trouble
    Ignatz on the Air
    Happy Birthday
    The Note
    Lucy
    Evidence
    Worse Than Nothing
    The Strange Object

CHAPTER FIVE 101
    Emptiness
    A Short Walk
    The Chance Meeting
    Cheddar Cheese

  Ignatz Returns
  His Protective Care
  Make Her Squirm
  Too Trusting

CHAPTER SIX..119
  The Crystal Ball
  Potato Salad on the Sleeves
  The Honest Tear
  Clippings
  Bell Trouble
  The Guest of Honor
  The Tar Bubble
  Almost Ready
  Good News!

CHAPTER SEVEN...141
  A Heavy Heart
  Music
  I Watch Him
  Starting Over
  The Boiling Point
  Bless Her Heart
  Public Rebuke

CHAPTER EIGHT..161
    The Reluctant Advisor
    Something You Should Know
    A Day to Remember
    Can It Last?

CHAPTER NINE...........…..........................177
    Tell Him
    Sweet Comfort
    Tilly on the Air
    The Hospital
    I Can Count
    Picketers
    Make Him Go Away

CHAPTER TEN..201
    Kindness
    The Dear Ruins
    The Supper
    A Brightness of Hope
    The Perfect Day

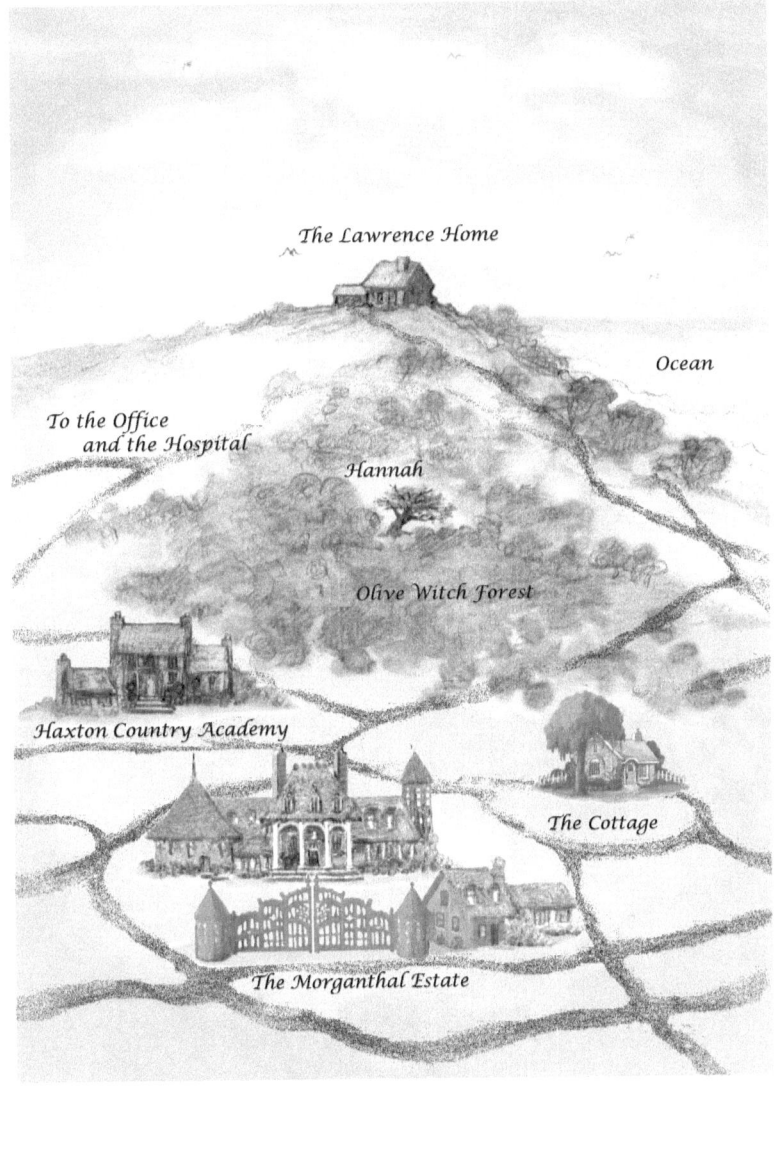

ILLUSTRATIONS

I think a couple's hopes are intertwined 5

Nothing could hide her humiliation 33

I never gone to no birthday party 81

Madame Vadoma's hands quivered artfully 123

You special, special people deserve the truth! 157

You see, you don't have a monopoly on gossip 185

Laughing at nothing and everything 215

CHARACTERS

Hetty, *Henrietta Anne Lawrence Morganthal*

Morgan Morganthal, *Hetty's husband*

Katrinka Wallace, *Morgan's former fiancée*

Joseph Ostler, *Katrinka's husband*

Max and Mimi Morganthal, *Morgan's parents*

Leaf Locke, *Hetty's biological father*

Marian, *young wife of Leaf Locke; Joseph's stepsister*

Anne Locke, *Leaf's deceased first wife*

Beverley Ignatz Gorman, *former Morganthal Circus employee*

Freydis Fairburn, *Hetty's aunt; sister to Leaf Locke*

Dan and Dora Lawrence, *Hetty's adoptive parents*

—This story takes place in the year 1964—

CHAPTER ONE

Intertwined

Morgan glanced at his watch. Hetty was counting on him to meet her at the radio station in half an hour. He paced to the cockpit and parted the curtains. The copilot made a move as if to give up his seat. "What can we do for you, Mr. Morganthal?"

Morgan's hand on his shoulder gave the man permission to stay as he was. "Not a thing. I just want to thank you again—both of you. It's not the first time you've come to my rescue."

"It's an honor, sir."

Morgan resisted the urge to look at his watch again, but the pilot sensed his concern. "We'll make it," he said. "And a car's waiting for you." Morgan flashed him a smile, and together they praised the steady tailwinds.

The copilot seemed reluctant to end the pleasantries. "I hear the U.S. team wants you in the glider competition," he said. "Think you'll do it?"

"No, I'll pass on this one—we'd have to miss our daughter's fourth birthday."

"Too bad. You hold a distance record, don't you?"

Morgan shook his head. "Not officially."

His glider was in mothballs, but he thought how happy Hetty would be if they could spend some time in the air. A thatch of hair fell across his forehead, hiding his serious dark eyes, and he returned to his seat.

Even during a short business trip like this one, he longed for Hetty and ached at their separation. The hint of a smile crinkled the corners his eyes, and he imagined himself soaring with her, high toward the brilliance of the sun—like eagles rising together above the clouds to a place of pure love.

The steam from Morgan's breath fogged the window, and he cleared it with his sleeve. As the plane descended through the clouds, he watched for their home. The lush forest that spread north of the cottage was easy to spot.

Many memories connected him to that piece of earth. The day before Morgan was to marry the beauty queen Katrinka Wallace, he knew he would find Hetty there in the forest. He sought her with the painful intention of saying goodbye. She was seventeen at the time.

When he found her she was in a tree, sobbing with a broken heart. What happened next changed everything. Hetty's desperate confessions of love astonished them both, forever blending their lives and dreams.

Twelve minutes after the plane touched down, the limousine delivered Morgan to the entrance of the radio station. The driver would deal with the luggage, and Morgan thanked him. As he sprinted up the steps, Morgan noticed the shine of the revolving doors. The *Morganthal* logo was spotless.

The manager was waiting. He appeared nervous until Morgan smiled and extended his hand. "Looking good, Joe," he said. Morgan suspected the cleaning crew scurried around in a panic whenever they heard he was coming. Still, they deserved his appreciation.

Together the men hurried to where Hetty stood outside the broadcast studio. Her cheeks colored with pleasure as Morgan approached, and his eyes drank in her unspoken

CHAPTER ONE

affection. "You must have been worried," he said. "I'm so sorry."

"No, not at all. I knew I could count on you." Her smile affirmed her confidence. Morgan saw no reason to mention having chartered the plane. Her lips were moist and sweet. She smelled like honeysuckle, and he wanted to be alone with her.

The manager lit the neon *quiet* sign with a snap and opened the door to the radio studio. "Let's go in," he said. "They're ready for you."

The microphones were on. Morgan sat across the table from Hetty. A short bald man waved an *applause* sign, and the audience clapped in response.

Hetty's long legs reached under the table close to Morgan. The lights played softly in the puffs of her pale hair. Leaning toward the microphone, she raised her eyes to meet his. "Welcome," she said, "to the first broadcast of *Hetty on Hold*. I'm Hetty Lawrence Morganthal."

Morgan wanted to grab her by the hand, run through the glorious spring sunshine, and take her home to the cottage. That's where they belonged. Not in this radio studio, with strangers gawking at him. He'd had enough of adoring fans that knew him from pictures in the society pages.

When the applause tapered off, Hetty continued. "This is a weekly show. Each Saturday I'll invite a guest to entertain or inform us," she said. "Today I'm honored to introduce my favorite person—and the owner of this station—successful businessman and attorney, Mr. Morgan Morganthal."

The applause was loud and sincere, but Morgan couldn't smile. The sweetness of her voice brought a lump to his throat. Hetty's trust in him was transparent.

Her ankle touched his. "We're fortunate to have you as our guest, Mr. Morganthal. Many of our listeners have been following your life and career. We look forward to hearing about your experiences. Or maybe your hopes and dreams."

Something in her tone seemed to invite a deep and personal honesty. If only he could read her mind! "You really mean it?" he asked.

"Yes, I do."

In no time, Hetty announced a commercial break. A noisy jingle about Whittlesey's Drug store followed.

During the interruption, Morgan felt sorry he and Hetty had no topics in mind to discuss. Soon after he had asked Hetty to host the talk show, legal problems threatened the Morganthal Circus. A deadlock halted the Ferris wheel negotiations, and Morgan had to catch a quick flight to solve it. He had been gone all six days since then.

Morgan's responsibility for running the immense Morganthal conglomerate kept him constantly in the public eye, so he was seldom at a loss for words. But for some reason all he could think of now was the sweet change Hetty had brought to his world.

Gratitude warmed his thoughts. He pictured their ivy-covered cottage . . . the wooden bench where they found shade under the rose trellis. They often sat there listening to the birds while Pippa picked violets. When it cooled at sundown, he would hold his family close to keep them warm. Sometimes the aroma of hot fresh bread drew them inside to the cozy kitchen. He and Pippa would watch Hetty slather honey butter on the thick, crusty slices.

Hetty had risked her life to have their child. The love they shared for Pippa was in stark contrast with the coldness of his childhood. His parents had shown little interest in him and his sister Melinda.

Hetty's voice signaled the end of the commercial, jolting Morgan from his thoughts. What was it she asked him? Oh, yes . . . she said it again . . . his hopes and dreams.

Morgan stroked his chin with his knuckles. "Don't you think this is risky interviewing your husband?"

Hetty smiled. "We'll know by the end of the hour."

I think a couple's hopes are intertwined.

He had expected her to ask about the new acrobatic act, or his plans for the elephant sanctuary—maybe his summers as a smokejumper. Shifting his weight, Morgan fixed his serious dark eyes on his wife.

He paused and breathed deeply. "I dream of my wife caring for our child at home," he said. "Wiping her tears and singing her to sleep. Helping her to grow up secure and happy."

Morgan surprised himself with his words. Maybe he was being selfish. He really didn't mean it that way.

Hetty's eyes widened, and she blinked rapidly. "Oh, yes . . . I see," she said. "But isn't that more about what you want your *wife's* dreams to be?"

"I suppose so," he said, "but I think a couple's hopes are intertwined." His honesty seemed to require further explanation. "Why would a wonderful mother take time off from what she enjoys and does so well?"

Hetty's hand tightened on the microphone. "Well, I know you love being a dad," she said, "but does that mean you can't perform with the Morganthal Circus? Or enter glider competitions?"

"You do have a point." The tone of his voice signaled a dead end.

Attempting a weak smile, Hetty began again. "So . . . you think we should only pursue the things we already do best? Isn't it good to try new things too?"

"Yes," he said, "but I wonder what Hetty's planning to put on hold. Is it her family? Her legal career? Maybe it's both."

"Oh, no! It just means I'm on hold while you talk. The microphone is all yours now. Today's program isn't supposed to be about me. It's about you."

"Fair enough," he said. "I'd be glad to explain something that happened to me a few years ago. It was 1955. An unbelievable summer. My father and I decided to shelter a baby chimp and a couple of our circus elephants. We hired a sweet young girl to help us. She worked with us every day,

CHAPTER ONE

shoveling elephant dung. She was shy and quiet, but she kept up with the work.

"It was the surprise of my life. I found myself bewitched—crazy in love."

Hetty's hands shook slightly, rustling the papers before her.

"I want to tell people what she did to me," he continued. "For years I was promised to someone else. Then the afternoon before the wedding, that teenager proposed to me. She threw the stars out of alignment.

"I'm talking about you. Now what kind of girl would do a thing like that? You'd think it was someone who wanted to be a wife and mother." The words came on his breath, to her alone. "I wanted to have you forever. So here we are—two lawyers in the same house." He touched her fingers. "Now we're married," he said softly, "and it still feels like a dream."

A muffled cough in the audience seemed to remind Morgan they were not alone. He straightened his back and grinned. "I've always thought you'd be at home with our daughter on a day like this, but instead, you've left her with two people who know nothing about children."

"Morgan! Our listeners must think your wife is impulsive and irresponsible."

"I'm sure they do," he said, "so let me explain. *I'm* the one who asked my parents to babysit." There was a short silence and a burst of laughter from the audience.

Morgan continued. "Tell me, do you really expect to keep this up?"

"What . . . what are you saying?"

"I wonder if you can do it," he said.

"But you're the one who asked me to!"

Morgan flashed her a smile. "You were the best choice, but I thought you'd say no. I just wish you hadn't been so enthusiastic."

She steadied her hands against the edge of the table. "My enthusiasm began," she said, "when you were willing to be my first guest."

"I wasn't willing," said Morgan. "You'll remember I suggested Katrinka Wallace should do this instead of me. In the future, what sort of guests do you want to have?"

"Not any one sort. Everyone's interesting inside. The adventure is in finding what makes them that way."

"Sounds like you want to keep this up."

"Well actually, yes. That is if my husband . . . or I mean my boss invites me to."

"As your husband, I want you home. As your boss, I'd be a fool not to hire you."

The hour passed quickly. The audience cheered before the bald man raised his sign. The show was over.

When the microphones were turned off, a group of girls approached Morgan for his autograph. The shy ones hung back a little, but when they put their papers and pens forward, he stood to put them at ease.

At last they whispered and giggled their way out of hearing, leaving Morgan and Hetty alone. For an awkward moment, Morgan frowned into space. "You should call this program *People Say Stupid Things*. Will you forgive me?"

Hetty stood and put her hand in his. "Well . . . you did stay on the subject," she said. "You told us your dreams."

He lowered his eyebrows. "I think I've needed your influence since you were twelve years old. Now suddenly you want to do this public thing," he said. "It's hard to share you. I'm not sure how I'm supposed to feel." His finger tapped the table. "Before I asked you to host the show, I heard Katrinka wanted the position. I almost gave it to her."

The color spread across Hetty's cheeks. "So . . . you almost gave it to Katrinka? If that's who you prefer, I'll understand."

Morgan took a deep breath. "No. Besides, I can't. I already told her you'd be taking over."

"Oh, I see . . . that puts you in a rather awkward spot."

CHAPTER ONE

"Yes," said Morgan, "but I've done it to myself. I fired Lambert so suddenly I had to think fast. It didn't give you much time, either."

"It was a surprise," said Hetty. "Lambert had a lot of fans. What was the matter?"

"Nothing," said Morgan. "Except his mouth," He looked up. "But I'd feel just as uneasy if *Katrinka* were hosting it. She's so unpredictable."

He seemed to recognize the irony of his words and inspected the floor apologetically. "Speaking of unpredictable," he said, "I know my comments threw you off guard. Please let me make up for it." His smile was kind. "Maybe I could take care of Pippa during the next show."

"Oh . . . Yes. Good," said Hetty. "Pippa would love it."

Visibly relieved, Morgan embraced her warmly. "Look out, world," he said. "Here comes Hetty!

"And about Katrinka," he added, "could you have her on the show right away? Just to make peace with her, you know."

"Katrinka?" Hetty's voice was weak.

"Right," he said. "People know she's a beauty queen. They'll tune in." A smile crinkled the corners of his eyes. "And they'll expect fireworks. That's her appeal."

The color drained from Hetty's face. She clenched the folds of her skirt and sat slowly.

Rice

Hetty was silent as they drove away from the radio show. She pressed her forehead against the vibrations of the window and looked out at nothing in particular.

Maybe Morgan would understand if she avoided talking just now. She leaned back and closed her eyes. It was easier to think that way.

Why am I so afraid of Katrinka Wallace? Maybe it's her breezy self-confidence. Exactly what I lack.

I ought to sympathize with her. She was so young when her father sent her to boarding school. She missed him terribly. Phil Wallace was such a dear man—just trying to do the right thing. He didn't want her friends to know he was a dwarf.

I mustn't resent Katrinka's connections with Morgan. It's not his fault. But I wonder if he understands how uncomfortable she makes me.

The car swung around a familiar curve. Hetty opened her eyes as they passed through the massive entrance to Max and Mimi Morganthal's estate. The guard saluted Morgan and lifted the bars to open the wrought iron gates. They entered and circled past the spacious gatehouse in which Katrinka Wallace lived with her husband, Joseph Ostler.

Beyond the gatehouse was the open stretch of lawn where Hetty and Morgan had received wedding guests almost four years ago. After the reception, rice was everywhere.

Rice, she thought. *The symbol of fertility. I forgot to notice if it sprouted. When we ran across the lawn to the car, people threw handfuls at us. It's supposed to wish newlyweds lots of babies. They meant well. No one knew I wasn't supposed to have any.*

Not ever.

Before their marriage, Morgan and Hetty endured a self-imposed distance. They remained apart four long years. Morgan needed to be sure her affection for him was more than a youthful crush.

When at last they were married, their years of waiting rewarded them with exultant gratitude. Confessing to the misery of their previous lovesick yearnings, they could marvel freely at the joys of respectful familiarity. In spite of concerns for Hetty's health, the rapture of discovery sweetened their union beyond imagining.

CHAPTER ONE

Pippa's birth came in celebration of their sacred intimacy. Rice had not been responsible.

The Phone Call

When Morgan stopped the car at his parents' front door, little Pippa stood in the marble entry. She wore a costly sun suit and matching sandals Max and Mimi Morganthal had purchased for her on the French Riviera. She had been waiting eagerly to show them, but above all to give them joyous hugs and moist kisses.

On the way home Hetty and Morgan listened to their daughter's cheerful chatter, and in no time they found themselves home at the cottage.

Pippa took Morgan's hand and skipped along the smooth stones to the front porch, but Hetty lagged behind them. With grim resolve, she entered through the open door and moved stiffly to the kitchen telephone.

For a brief moment she closed her eyes. Her fingers gripped the receiver tightly, and she dialed Katrinka.

"Oh, Hetty, my *dearest* friend!" said Katrinka. "I'm so glad you called. I listened to the whole program, and you were absolutely adorable. I wanted to jump up and down and let the whole world know you're my attorney. I was so proud of you!

"I knew my name would come up. If it hadn't, someone from the audience would have mentioned me anyway. Morgan and I made such a fabulous looking couple for so long.

"I can't believe how beastly he was to you. My Joseph would *never* have done anything like that. Of course it's because he *adores* me. But we can't all be so lucky."

Hetty twisted the telephone cord. Her breathing was shallow and rapid as she listened.

"I think you're amazingly brave," said Katrinka. "Especially since you know less than nothing about hosting a radio show.

But it might not be so obvious to the average person. Hetty, you've simply *got* to loosen up! You could have come to me for advice, you know. I've had so much experience before the public. The difference is that *I* of course prefer the *camera*. If color television ever gets popular, I might even want my own TV show some day.

"For now, isn't it a blessing you're on radio, and nobody can see you? I just mean this is the sixties, for heaven's sake," said Katrinka. "You need to get with the times. And your hair! Bless your heart, it's so totally unmanageable. Don't you need to cut it or something? You know, because of Pippa. A normal three-year-old would be pulling on it. But maybe she's a little behind in her development.

"Joseph and I don't want a family. At least *I* don't. I don't even want to adopt. I can't imagine how you cope with being adopted, you poor thing. It's a wonder you can even remember Leaf Locke is your real father. I mean the way you thought Dan and Dora Lawrence were your parents. I'm sure everybody else could tell you were adopted. It's so obvious, what with you being so much taller.

"My Joseph doesn't see what's so complicated about the whole mess. You must admit it's odd having two entire sets of parents who are all chummy, when I don't have any living parents at all!

"Don't get me wrong. I think it's the sweetest thing ever, the way Dan lets you and Morgan practice law with him. Really I do.

"Obviously Morgan could have done better," she said, "but I realize you didn't go to Harvard like him. I suppose Dan was worried about his little girl not getting in any other firm." She laughed sweetly, perhaps to demonstrate how charming cruelty could be when delivered with a sense of humor. "So what if they didn't accept women! All it takes is a little gumption and a certain *je ne sais quoi*. If it was me, *I* would have found a way.

CHAPTER ONE

"Anyway," she said, "I can't imagine it working out very long. Family businesses can get pretty nasty, if you know what I mean.

"I'm only saying these things to let you know my heart is with you. I understand how much you have to overcome. I feel these things more deeply than other people.

"I hope this little talk has been helpful to you," she said. "I'll always be your friend. I feel so much better when I confide in you."

Katrinka sighed with a depth matched only by the sensitivity of her soul.

"Anyway, if I had children, I'm sure they'd be real smart like my Daddy. Most likely they'd be dwarfs like him. I miss him terribly. I wish I could talk to him. Everything would be better if Daddy was still alive."

"Yes," said Hetty. "We all miss Phil." After a tactful silence, she continued. "I called you, because I wondered . . . I mean I'm hoping you'll be my guest on the next program."

There was a long pause followed by Katrinka's sweetest musical voice. "Tell me, Hetty dear," she cooed, "Whose idea was it?

"Hetty?" There was more silence. "I thought so," said Katrinka. "It was Morgan who wanted me." The triumph broke her laughter into icy splinters.

"We both want you to do it," said Hetty. "You know how to get people's attention."

"Of course I do, Hetty darling." Katrinka's frozen words rang like little bells. "That's why you need me."

The phone call was over. Hetty hung up the telephone and stared at the floor. Pippa stood next to Morgan in the wingback chair with one arm around her father's neck. She hummed and folded his earlobe up and down.

Hetty waited, as if reluctant to disturb the scene, but Morgan closed his newspaper and turned toward her. Hetty moved to his side and fingered his other earlobe with unnatural cheerfulness. "Katrinka will do it," she said.

Morgan nodded. "I hope you're all right with it." He listened for her reply. "Are you?"

"I don't know," said Hetty.

"Why not? Is it because of the way I asked?" he said. "Did you call her because you thought I left you no choice?"

Pippa hopped to the floor and stuffed the newspaper under the chair.

"I'm not sure," said Hetty. "It's not your fault I wanted to please you, Morgan."

"Let's think then," he laughed. "Who should we blame?"

"Well," she stammered, "I think sometimes there *is* a fine line between . . . between suggesting and manipulating."

Morgan jolted forward and pulled the crumpled paper out from under the chair. He didn't pretend to look at it. "So you feel what—controlled?"

She bit her lip. "Maybe I used too strong a word."

He paused, and silence controlled the space around him. His hands jerked as he smoothed the rumpled newspaper across his lap. "Not necessarily," he said. "Not if you meant it." His unwavering gaze was a question mark hanging in the air. Neither one knew the answer. He lowered his eyebrows. "You can make your own decisions about what you want," he said. He paused again and inspected the smudges of newsprint on his fingers.

"Here's what I think is going on," he said. "We come from two different families. The guidance from your parents—no matter how subtle it was, you learned from it. I didn't get any guidance. Except for the bruises, and getting knocked around a little. Dad used the direct approach, and you could say I took it on the chin.

"Of course Phil Wallace was like a father," he said. "But I couldn't stay with him when he toured with the circus." He turned his hands up again.

CHAPTER ONE

Hetty sat on the arm of his chair. "Everything is a balancing act, isn't it? Between the office and Pippa and shopping and cooking and laundry and gardening," she sighed. "And other things. It's hard to get it right."

He smiled. "Yes, it's the other things," he said. "Knowing what matters most, so we don't get too busy for what's important." He opened his mouth as if to soften his words, but Hetty stood and put her hands in his.

"Don't let the newsprint rub off on you," he said.

Hetty leaned closer. "You say I should make my own decisions about what I want." Her lips parted in a smile. "Please Morgan, I want everything about you to rub off on me."

"And you," he said, "the way Dan and Dora raised you—with absolute love—that's what I want for us and our children."

He caught himself quickly. "That is our . . . Pippa."

In Recovery

It was Saturday afternoon. Max and Mimi Morganthal were exhausted. Pippa had been with them during Hetty's broadcast because no one else could tend her that morning. They sat on the edge of the bed and removed their shoes.

"I wonder how Hetty does it," said Mimi.

Max stretched out on the silk brocade coverlet and looked up at the immense crystal chandelier. "So do I." He closed his eyes.

Mimi laid her hand on his chest. "I wish Swenson hadn't retired. He knew how to keep her occupied. Pippa felt grown up, helping him polish silver." She sighed. "It's been hard enough losing the chauffeur. And now the butler."

Max opened his eyes. "I can see why people our age stop having children."

"But just think," said Mimi. "Hetty's father Leaf is almost fifty. He and Marian have Danny."

Max put his hands behind his head. "Well, Marian's younger. She has the energy, if not the competence."

"True," said Mimi. "She's no better at parenting than we were. But at least she tries, which is more than we did."

Max nodded in agreement. They both regretted their neglect of Morgan and Melinda. At an early age, Morgan had taken responsibility for his little sister. His attention to her was probably all that kept the family together.

Mimi's eyes wandered over the perfection of her husband's chiseled features. She sighed as if enjoying the tranquility. "Max," she said, "I don't know how we could have been invisible to each other for twenty years."

He laughed. "It was insane—like two blind people in the same house trying not to bump into each other."

"Yes," she said, "we owe a lot to Hetty. If it hadn't been for her, we'd still be living that way."

He chuckled. "We're making up for it, aren't we?"

Mimi smiled and looked up at the cupids painted on the ceiling. "Before long, we'll be on the beach in Jamaica," she said.

Max propped himself up beside her. "After we get there, I'll have to leave you for the day. The tourism board in Kingston wants my advice. Morgan says it won't take long. I'll set you up in the hotel first. The concierge will give you whatever you need. And I've arranged for a driver," he said. "Don't you worry. Soon as we're home from Jamaica, I promise we'll find a replacement for Swenson."

Mimi gave him a tender smile. "Until then," she said, "I like being alone with you."

CHAPTER ONE

The Letter

Leaf and Marian Locke never had the problem of losing servants. For that matter, they never had servants. Leaf's career as a botany professor did not suggest that sort of luxury, and Marian, by her own account, worked at the library more for pleasure than for profit. It was unusual for work to occupy an entire Saturday as it had today.

They both regretted being unable to care for Pippa that morning. Leaf was as entranced with his granddaughter as he was with his own sturdy five-year-old son Danny. Little Pippa was a slender wisp—a small image of her mother Hetty—and so very like Anne, his first wife. Anne had passed down her pale lashes and translucent skin to them both.

Anne's hair had been soft as the down of milkweed, and she had eyes blue as the summer sky. Leaf kept a picture of her hidden in his bottom drawer, under his winter shirts.

Soon after walking in the door, Leaf preheated the oven for the peach pie he had prepared that morning, and Marian went to the mailbox with Danny. She lifted him to see what treasures it contained. Though his big sister Hetty lived in the same town, sometimes she sent him real letters, because he was getting big and would soon be in kindergarten.

Leaf waited at the door for his two redheads. Danny carried the stack of mail back to the house with help from his mother. "I'm the mailman, Daddy. You can be Mr. Locke."

Leaf got down on one knee. "All right, Mr. Mailman. Anything for me?"

The minute Danny discovered a postcard from Hetty, he lost interest in the game and skipped away with it.

"Leaf," said Marian, "here's one from Freydis." He inspected the envelope. "That's odd. It's from England, all right. But this isn't my sister's handwriting."

Leaf moved toward the kitchen to find a knife, walking slowly, as if reluctant to open it. His large gray eyes were soft and kind. Marian held her breath and watched his long slender fingers turn the pages.

He moved his tall frame to stand silently beside her. Together they looked out the window until it was time for words.

"About Freydis," he said. "She's had a stroke."

Marian slipped her arms around him. "Oh, Leaf, I'm so sorry. I know she's much more than a sister to you."

He fixed his gaze out the window. "She's twenty years older than I am. Still, I wasn't prepared for this. At least she was living out her dream. As long as I can remember, she's wanted to spend time in England—Stratford-upon-Avon, The Globe Theatre . . . " His voice trailed off.

"How bad is it?"

"Apparently she's more frail and a little confused," he said. "Sometimes she forgets her husband's dead. And she's been imagining impossible stories."

Leaf looked down into Marian's brown eyes and freckled face. "Freydis wants to come home and live with me again in the cottage," he said. "She doesn't understand it can never be the same. It can't work with Morgan and Hetty living there now. And she forgets you and I are married."

Leaf anticipated Marian's thoughts and stroked her red hair.

"Leaf, I'm frightened," she said. "You know I love Freydis." Her voice was unsteady. "She ought to live with us, but I don't think I can do it." She put her head against his chest.

Across the room, Danny faced a cowboy puppet that was hopelessly tangled in its own strings. Its head drooped to one side, so Danny leaned it against a boot. Standing over the little figure, he instructed it to pay attention. Then to the best of his ability, Danny read aloud the greeting on Hetty's postcard.

CHAPTER ONE

Keeping Score

Leaf unfolded the letter about Freydis, but he knew it wouldn't change anything to read it again. Marian would still worry. He sat on the edge of the bed and tapped the envelope on his knee.

Leaning forward, he opened the bottom drawer of his dresser to put the letter away. He laid it on top of his plaid flannel shirt, but instead of closing the drawer, he felt under the folded clothes until his fingers held the rim of a picture frame.

"Anne," he whispered. That was all he wanted to say, really. But his hands were eager to pull out the photograph and hold it, if only for a minute or two. As he tilted the frame, Anne's eyes seemed to follow him. He would have hidden the picture again, but something about her expression encouraged him to speak.

"What are we going to do?" He sought answers in the blue eyes looking back at him. Though her voice was seldom clear in his memory, the sound of it now seemed to speak to his thoughts.

"I will always love you, Leaf." She seemed to say it with a little sigh the way she had when she was alive.

Leaf smiled. "I know," he said. "Some things go on forever." He checked the back of the frame and tightened a small screw with his fingernail.

"I wish I could help," said Anne. "I agree Freydis should live here, but would it be fair to Marian? It's hard enough for her, just taking care of Danny."

Suddenly, her eyes brightened. "Oh, Leaf, what a wonderful child he is! I wonder—maybe in time Marian won't be so overwhelmed. When does Danny start kindergarten?"

"He'll be going this fall, and I'll miss him terribly." Leaf looked out the window at the swing set. "Do you think I should keep helping Marian with the cooking?"

"You never helped me with the cooking."

"Did you want me to?"

"Not really." Leaf loved the way Anne's brown eyes shone when she smiled. Or maybe it was Marian's eyes he was picturing. Anne's were blue as the sky.

He could hear her voice again. "Remember when we used to play Scrabble?" she said. "I'd be stirring a pot at the stove, but I'd run back to the game when it was my turn."

Leaf chuckled. "Marian is even better at Scrabble, but she doesn't keep score like you."

No matter what game they played, Anne always kept score in a little red notebook. Or was her notebook blue? He couldn't remember.

"Marian probably thinks it would be hard on your pride," she said.

"If you had lived," thought Leaf, "would you have found it hard to be a wife and mother? As hard as it is for Marian?"

Anne flopped down on the bed, and her eyes narrowed with amusement.

"You'll never know, will you?"

She held onto the bedpost, floating and swirling lightly around it. Leaf wanted to reach for her, to become entangled in her glorious red hair and feel it shimmer in his fingers. Or maybe he was thinking of Marian's hair. Yes, of course. Anne's hair was pale like Hetty's.

Anne floated behind him so he couldn't imagine her as well. "I have an idea," she said. "You could pretend homemaking was just as hard for me as it is for Marian. On the other hand, does it really matter? You love her anyway."

Leaf nodded. "You have a point," he said.

CHAPTER ONE

"Thank you." Anne held up her little notebook. "That's one point for me," she said. She recorded the score with her finger and hummed something he couldn't identify.

Anne cocked her head. "You wondered if I would always be tone deaf," she said.

Leaf raised his eyebrows. "How did you know?"

She laughed and clapped her hands. "I didn't. You just now thought of it yourself."

"Well, it really didn't matter," he thought, "because I loved you." Anne smiled and produced the spiral notebook again. Her finger recorded one point for Leaf.

"I've been thinking," she said. "Marian has a good ear for music. If you fiddle for her, she'll probably yodel like she did before you were married." Anne looked pensive. "I love Marian," she said, "because she makes you happy."

Leaf indicated the notebook, and Anne added another point with her finger. She spoke quietly to herself. "A point for me is a point for you is a point for Marian is a point for Danny is a point for Hetty . . ." Her voice trailed off. "That's how it works."

Leaf laughed to himself. "Anne's right. That's how it works.

"Marian may always be a little insecure," he thought. "Her mother taught her never to trust men. It's a wonder she trusts anyone."

Leaf was startled to hear Marian approach from behind. His thoughts ended abruptly, and Anne's picture clattered to the floor.

"Oh! I didn't mean to surprise you." Marian sounded quite breathless with embarrassment. She watched Leaf pick up the picture and put it in the drawer. The glass hadn't broken.

The phone rang, and Marian appeared relieved by the excuse to escape such an awkward moment. It was Hetty wondering if her little brother had received the postcard, and her voice triggered Marian's tears.

"Are you all right?" asked Hetty.

Marian sobbed softly. "I don't know," she said.

Hetty waited for her stepmother to recover, but that didn't seem likely anytime soon. "Do you need me?" she asked.

Marian wiped away her tears and whispered into the phone. "I'm mad at your father," she said. "Why does he keep Anne's picture? I wanted to be enough for him. When we first got married, I hoped he might try to forget her. Do I have to share him forever?"

When Marian seemed ready to listen, Hetty spoke. "I guess . . . I honestly hope so," she said. "If he'd married you first, of course he'd never forget *you*. He wouldn't want to. Everything that's happened to Father could only make him understand and care about you even more. His life is so full of you and Danny that it spills over to me, and I'm glad."

Hetty took a deep breath and began again. "It doesn't mean he loves you any less just because of me. Love doesn't get used up in the exercise of it. I think it grows, instead.

"And isn't it harder to love somebody when you're angry at the same time? I don't like that feeling."

"I know," whispered Marian, "I know."

It was quiet, and Hetty asked, "Are you still there?" Her words went unanswered. Marian dropped the phone as Leaf kissed a tear from her cheek.

Anne would have reason to add a point to everyone's score.

Family Conference

It was a peaceful Sunday afternoon. The lazy sun slanted through the windows. Hetty had put away the leftovers, but the cottage still bore the scent of buttered potatoes and Yorkshire pudding. Leaf had called earlier to ask if they could meet as a family. Both sets of her parents would arrive soon.

CHAPTER ONE

Hetty leaned into the curve of the piano and looked outside to the garden. A robin flew to the climbing roses over the gate, and a squirrel hid an acorn in the moss beneath the ferns. But Hetty's gaze followed Morgan. Her countenance softened with an expression reserved for him alone, and her eyes were misty. Perhaps it was the memories they had made together.

She wanted to deserve his approval now as much as ever. The very thought of Morgan made Hetty reach for whatever was fine and good. Maybe she still wondered how her dreams of him could have become reality.

She watched Pippa run to her father from the far corner of the yard, her soft curls dancing and her arms reaching. Morgan lifted her to the strong support of his shoulders. There was a natural grace and ease to his movements.

Phil Wallace had recognized those gifts and trained him in the ways of the circus at an early age. Morgan was at home on an elephant or a dancing horse. He could juggle with a steady hand or perform on a unicycle. Yet he appeared most at ease here in the cottage garden with Pippa.

Firm and steady, maybe he was born to stand facing the forest and the clouds with a child who laughed and gripped his dark hair with her pudgy fingers. It seemed to Hetty that Morgan had been created for just such a moment.

Hetty's adoptive parents, Dan and Dora Lawrence, arrived first. Soon, Hetty's father Leaf entered with his wife Marian and their son Danny.

"I hope they recorded your program yesterday," said Marian.

Hetty avoided a direct answer. "There's always next week," she said.

Dan gave a shiny penny to his young namesake and another to his granddaughter Pippa. It reminded Hetty of when she had been their age. Papa Dan's eyes were smiling and he honked his nose into a large red handkerchief like the one she remembered.

The adults gathered in the dining room, and when the six of them were seated, Leaf spread the open letter on the table. He explained what he learned of Freydis the day before.

"We need a plan," he said. He looked at his good friend. "I think I should quote you, Dan: *'Gather the facts, and the decisions will make themselves.'* You've said it many times."

Dan nodded, and Leaf looked at their daughter. "I'm sorry, Hetty dear," he said. "I wish I didn't have to involve you." He shifted his long legs under the table.

Morgan faced his father-in-law squarely. "If I may, before you go on—there's no reason you should apologize. Things like this happen."

Hetty was the next one to address Leaf. "I can understand why she wants to live here. We all love our memories in this place. I'm sure she remembers the music we all made together." She sought Morgan's hand under the table. "And Aunt Freydis bought this place with you, Father."

Leaf nodded. "I didn't want her to be a widow living alone." He looked at his wife.

Marian mentioned another complication. "Your Aunt Freydis has some hearing loss too," she said.

Hetty glanced at the children under the piano in the sunroom. Pippa was crooning a lullaby to the dump truck she cradled in her arms. Danny drummed noisily on an oatmeal box with Pippa's doll. Hetty said, "A little hearing loss could be a blessing."

Dan Lawrence remembered he was supposed to bring Dora's oatmeal chocolate chip cookies in from the car. While he went for them, Morgan poured some tall glasses of milk.

The family nibbled and talked until Marian took a deep breath. "I think Freydis is our responsibility. She's my sister-in-law, and I think she should stay with us." She spoke bravely, but her unsteady voice betrayed her.

CHAPTER ONE

The firm grip of Morgan's hand gave Hetty the courage to answer. She spoke to Marian, her stepmother and dear friend. "Why don't we see how it works here first?" she said. "We want her to live with us."

So it was decided, and Marian was visibly relieved.

Hetty looked around quietly. The cottage had many small but inviting gathering places. She loved the sunny corners that encouraged thoughtful conversation, the cushioned seat in the bay window where she read to Pippa.

She thought of the quiet moments alone with Morgan, when his breath was on her cheek. The climbing roses by the front gate would always nod in the breeze, but would she ever again have time to notice?

While Morgan said good-bye at the door, Hetty removed herself to the bathroom and wept in secret.

CHAPTER TWO

Sweet Victory

It didn't seem like a week since the first *Hetty on Hold,* but Saturday came as it always did. Hetty had left early in the morning. Today's interview would be with Katrinka.

At home in the cottage, Morgan held Pippa on his lap. Leaning forward in his armchair, he adjusted the knob of the radio with precision. Morgan had thought of everything possible to keep Pippa quietly occupied so he could listen. Toys encircled their chair like a moat designed to keep a princess in her castle.

The program began with loud applause and whistles. Then came Hetty's clear voice. "Welcome to *Hetty on Hold,*" she said. "I'm Hetty Morganthal. Would you please welcome today's guest, the beautiful Katrinka Wallace!"

The whistles increased, and Hetty interrupted the audience before it reached the point of rudeness. "Miss Wallace is the chief operating officer of LuvCon, formerly known as Luvliness Conglomerates," she said.

Pippa squealed at her mother's voice. "Mommy!" she said, sliding from Morgan's lap. "I want Mommy!"

"She'll be home soon, honey."

"Okay," she said. "I get Mommy outside." She skipped over the moat to the front door. In no time, she was outside at the picket fence peeking through the climbing roses.

"Take my hand, Pippa. We need to go in again."

"Why?" She stooped down to pick a primrose growing between steppingstones.

"So you can put your flower in a vase," he said. She clutched two of his fingers and hopped over the soft mosses along the pathway.

When they opened the cottage door, Morgan heard Katrinka's musical voice. "You see, Hetty dear," she said, "A beautiful woman mustn't allow false modesty to control her tongue."

Pippa dragged a chair to the sink and floated her flower in a frying pan. As the kitchen clatter increased, Morgan leaned closer to the radio.

Katrinka continued. "You see, I've learned to succeed by using every gift I was born with."

With an intimate whisper to the audience, she said, "For those of you who have forgotten, Morgan Morganthal and I go way back. Our fathers were best friends growing up and they had a real famous clown act." Her voice quavered artfully with her next proclamation. "Morgan chose to break the promise he made to me when I was a trusting nine-year-old."

Morgan rolled his eyes and slumped back in the chair.

Katrinka sniffed. "I was betrayed. He cast me aside to marry someone else." The audience rustled and squirmed at the drama.

There was a brief silence before Hetty attempted a calm response. "I believe our listeners are aware I'm Mrs. Morgan Morganthal," she said, "and your husband, Joseph Ostler, is a fine man."

"Yes, Hetty darling. So now we come to my point. Who is the winner? *I* have a devoted and steadfast husband who *adores* me." Her little sigh was both sweet and triumphant. "And I reside with him in the gatehouse of the Maximilian

CHAPTER TWO

Morganthal estate. You know what an *elegant* setting that is. Honestly, I think *you* might have felt a wee bit out of place there."

Katrinka began again, more sympathetically this time. "Most people don't choose the simple life unless they have to. But it's back to nature, in your quaint little cottage. Bless your heart, you made your bed, and now you have to lie in it. Oh well, I'm happy for you anyway." She laughed sweetly. "Really I am!"

Morgan stared at the radio.

"Daddy?" said Pippa.

He covered his face with his hands.

"Daddy, I want more lollipop."

"More what?" he asked. He was straining to hear Hetty. "Just a minute, Pippa."

"Like this one, Daddy. 'Nother red one." She pulled at a lump stuck in her hair.

"Wait! Wait, honey, I'll get a washcloth for your hands. Don't worry, I can get it out."

The damp cloth arrived too late. Her fingers had lodged the sticky mass against her scalp.

"Stay here while I get the scissors. No, let's see . . . " He looked around the kitchen. "Yes, here . . . hold this cup in your hands."

"But there's no cocoa in it."

"Pretend there is, for just a minute," he said.

Tears gathered in Pippa's eyes." I don't want pretend cocoa," she wailed.

Morgan soon returned with lukewarm cocoa and a pair of scissors. "Hold still like a statue," he said, snipping around the sticky candy. "Good girl." He listened for Hetty's response.

"Please, Miss Wallace," she began, "tell our listeners about your role at LuvCon."

"Well, in all modesty, I'm considered the darling of the Morganthal business empire. You're familiar with the slogan I created. You see I believe 'Beauty is a gift we owe our loved ones.' That's what motivates my work. It's what I live by."

That evening when Hetty walked in the door, Pippa was already in her high chair at the kitchen table. "Mommy! I made a yummy, yummy dinner!"

There was something odd about her hair. Hetty glanced at the scissors on the counter.

Morgan looked exhausted, but he rose and held Hetty close. For some time they stood this way as if to draw quiet comfort from each other.

Supper began quietly. Pippa put a Brussels sprout in her mouth, but immediately let it fall to her plate and inspected it with suspicion. She continued her meal only when she had carefully covered the offending item with a heap of corned beef hash.

Morgan reached for Hetty's hand, and they laughed together at the cleverness of the child they had made together.

The Dream

Hetty couldn't sleep. She struggled to erase the memory of her interview with Katrinka earlier in the day, but it played over and over in her mind. When at last she lost all awareness of Morgan's steady breathing, her eyelids became heavy, and dreams overcame her consciousness.

She was standing in the center of a stage. Behind her, a flight of stairs rose to the sky through an opening in the ceiling. A glorious prize awaited inside a door at the top. It would be hers to take home if she could answer a few questions correctly.

Confident of winning, Hetty could hardly wait for the contest to start. When only one word of the first question appeared on the wall, she answered it correctly without waiting to see the rest of it.

CHAPTER TWO

Suddenly she noticed someone standing beside her. It was Katrinka Wallace. "Isn't it better to see the whole thing first?" asked Katrinka.

Hetty glanced up at the wall. She was already pleased with her performance and eager for another question. "Oh, no," she said, "Whatever the question is, I'll know the answer."

Katrinka's turn was next. She tried to read the question that appeared on the wall, but after puzzling over it, she said, "I'm not sure it's right the way I'm reading it. My little pea brain is still trying to figure it out, you know."

"I'm sure it is," said Hetty. "Right, I mean."

"What did you say?" asked Katrinka.

"I meant to say I think you're probably reading it correctly. Although your little brain is the size of a pea, I wasn't agreeing that you were still using it."

Katrinka frowned suspiciously before she continued. The next question had a long word in it, so she waited for another one that might be easier to read.

While she stalled, she applied some glossy pink lipstick and posed to look as alluring as possible.

Upon seeing the next question, she clapped her hands. "Hetty darling," she cooed, "This one is insanely simple. It's perfect for you." She smiled sweetly. "You'd have to be an absolute idiot to miss it!" Her blood-red fingernails looked especially pointy and appeared to grow longer. "I can even read it to you," she said.

"All right," said Hetty. This was going to be outrageously fun.

Katrinka looked up at the door. "Now don't worry," she said. "If you get it wrong, the prize won't go to waste." She tossed her hair and displayed her pearly-white teeth. "Because I'm here."

With her chin high in the air, she read the question. "Who

designed the wedding dress Elizabeth Taylor wore when she married Richard Burton?"

Suddenly, a diamond tiara appeared on Katrinka's head as a reminder that no movie star could compete with her matchless beauty. The audience sighed in unison at her loveliness.

Hetty gasped. Her hands felt cold and sweaty, and she tried to remember to breathe. "Oh, I . . . I thought the question would be about current affairs."

Katrinka laughed triumphantly. "And that's exactly what it is," she said. "A current affair." Her long eyelashes fanned the air, setting off a cool breeze.

The chill Hetty felt made her look down at herself for the first time. How could she have forgotten to put clothes on over her slip! A torn section of lace drooped down from the front hem. When someone in the audience pointed at her and snickered, others joined in, laughing.

She slumped forward, hoping her hair would cover as much as possible, but nothing could hide her humiliation. Hetty was perspiring with embarrassment. Her hair stuck to the tears on her cheeks, and her nose ran. Crouching in the corner, she hoped the lights and camera would find another target.

The scorching footlights beamed their suffocating heat directly on her. Her sobs echoed through the studio, and she realized the microphone cord had tightened its grip around her neck.

With a sudden drumroll, the door concealing the prize at the top of the stairway slowly opened. A hush fell over the audience as a magnificent man stepped through the opening. He looked toward Hetty.

Katrinka snatched a microphone and announced, "Ladies and gentlemen, the prize we've all been waiting for! The one and only Morgan Morganthal!"

Several girls in the audience fainted upon hearing his name. Others screamed and wept at the sight of him.

With the grace of a panther leaping from a tree, Morgan

Nothing could hide her humiliation.

swung from a rope and landed next to Hetty. He raised his hand to protect her eyes from the lights.

Hetty felt sick, knowing Morgan had seen her pride and the ugliness of her feelings about Katrinka. But he would be too kind to mention his disappointment. Hetty felt her heart would burst with sorrow.

"You were amazing," whispered Morgan. "The winner, for sure." He wiped her nose with his handkerchief.

Hetty trembled. "Do you really think so?" she asked.

"Well," he said, "I suppose I should ask Katrinka. She knows more about these things."

He walked across the stage to Katrinka and whispered, "Please don't let Hetty make a fool of herself."

Hetty held onto the heavy velvet stage curtains for support. When she pulled a little too hard, they fell in a heap around her. Thrashing around desperately, she became entangled in them.

She crouched there perspiring, thirsty, and trying to breathe. Wiping her tears on a corner of the curtain, she closed her eyes tightly so the audience would all go away.

"I'm sorry, Morgan," chortled Katrinka, "but the poor thing doesn't even know enough to push back her cuticles."

Morgan lowered his dark eyebrows. The females in the audience who had not already swooned did so now. He seemed unaware of the commotion and continued negotiating on Hetty's behalf.

"Well, I don't know much about cuticles either," he said.

Katrinka sighed. "Well, I just mean she's not one of us. But I'll do my best."

"Thank you, Katrinka," he said. "I'm indebted to you."

"You've always been indebted to me, Morgan honey. You just didn't know it." Katrinka assumed a tolerant, yet sympathetic, expression. "How did this ever happen, Morgan?"

"What do you mean?"

Katrinka laughed sweetly. "Well, you poor darling! You

could have had me," she said. "I'm the one with that certain 'je ne sais quoi.' I suppose you thought someone with a clean slate could learn. But Hetty's slate was a little too clean, bless her heart." She pursed her lips. "You thought she had so much potential, and that she'd be a fabulous mother who would give you ten or twelve children and make a real lovey-dovey home."

"Oh, I don't know," said Morgan, staring into space.

"Well, you must know why you married her."

"I forget. But it will come to me," he mused. "Maybe it doesn't matter."

Hetty cried quietly and held the curtain against her face.

Katrinka winked. "But it does, Morgan honey. You're a prominent man, and she needs to represent you better."

Morgan looked mournfully into the corner where Hetty huddled. "She's fine the way she is," he said uncertainly.

The announcer declared no one had won the prize.

Hetty felt a gust of fresh air. She took a gasping breath and opened her eyes. Her pillow was soggy with tears and perspiration. She was flooded with joyful relief at the sight of Morgan lying beside her. His deep sleep and steady breathing surprised her.

Though the nightmare had left Hetty tense and exhausted, she didn't dare close her eyes again. The dream would repeat itself as long as she felt anger toward Katrinka.

Whoopty-do

The airport in Kingston, Jamaica was all but deserted. Max wanted to join Mimi in Montego Bay, and he was accustomed to getting what he wanted. He was willing to charter a plane or take any available flight, but there was nothing. He squared his jaw and suppressed his anger.

His expression softened when a smallish dog with a sweet,

soulful face limped toward him. Someone had hand-carved a splint for her left front leg. One ear stood erect while the other luffed to the side like a fragile sail.

She looked up at Max and wagged her tail as if inviting him to stroke her smooth tan coat; however, her collar bore the words, "Keep your mitts off," followed by the initials "B.I.G."

Max watched the dog sniff at his leather suitcase until a man with greasy hair called out in a coarse voice. "Hey, Lucy ... hey!" He lurched toward her and picked up the dog with a gentleness that belied his rough appearance.

As the man straightened, his attention was on the rich brown leather bag next to Max. His eyes widened at the name *Morganthal* on the brass nameplate. After glancing furtively at Max, he sauntered away to pose dramatically against the wall. Soon he gave up, perhaps because Lucy's affectionate demeanor contributed nothing to the mysterious effect he was attempting. Besides, nobody noticed him even after he spat manfully into the corner.

After a thorough look at Max, he called out, "Hey! You stuck here?"

"Why?" said Max. "You know a way out?"

"Sure do," he said. He came close, rubbing his fingers together to signal his love of money. "It'll cost you," he said.

"Right," said Max. "Lead the way." They walked until the airport was far behind them. "What happened to your dog?"

"Huh?" Lucy nestled in her owner's arms and wagged her tail. "Oh, that. She got butted by one of them goats like we got too much of here," he said. "She can't get around too good. I like to show her stuff from my plane. She barks at the monkeys when we fly real low over the jungle."

They kept up a steady pace. Max shifted his suitcase to the other hand so he could reach out and feel Lucy's silky ears.

They reached an airplane that crouched in a field of weeds. Cables drooped from its only engine and flowed to

CHAPTER TWO

a generator, which sputtered on the timid support of four cinderblocks. Max stumbled up the steps to board the plane, ducked his head, and squeezed through the opening.

A single passenger seat had been fastened to the floor at one time, but the bolts had long since ripped loose, leaving holes in the plywood underfoot. Strips of wrinkled duct tape secured the window against the door panel. The pilot kicked at something and banged around with a wrench.

Before long they were airborne. As the plane roared through the clouds, it lurched and dipped. Max clutched the handle of his suitcase with one hand, his stomach with the other, and peered through the holes at the jungle below.

"Tell me about your airplane," he yelled.

"Huh? Well, it's like this, see. I got me this customer what owed me money. He practically *give* me this here plane. Just 'cause she ain't legal, so to speak. Leastwise not on a real airstrip, see." He shook his head. "And some idiot guy says I'm s'posed to get scads of practice before I can fly. Ha! What do you call this I'm doing now, for crying out loud!"

"Well, I know there are regulations," said Max. "My son put in a lot of airtime before he got his license."

"Whoopty-do. *Sounds* like Morgan."

"Oh! You know my son?"

"Me? Nah! You musta said his name."

Max breathed slowly in and out. His face looked a little green. "Mimi . . ." he mumbled, "my wife . . . she's waiting for me." He tried to raise his voice, doubting he had been heard. "I guess we'll make it there, right?"

"Yeah, sure," said the pilot. He reamed the wax from his ear with his index finger and became silent.

"Well," said Max, "I'm impressed you fly so your dog can see the world."

"Hey, she ain't no ordinary dog! I'm a business consecutive like you, and Lucy's my partner. She's real smart with the customers."

Lucy looked drowsily at Max from her position on the pilot's lap.

"I'll bet she is."

After a while the man spoke again. "Uh, I been consternating . . . maybe you could help me fix Lucy's leg. Like if I was working for you back in the States?"

Max stared through the holes in the floor as if to ignore the bold request, but looked up when Lucy sneezed. Her little pink tongue peeked out from the corner of her mouth, and she cocked her head. Perhaps she was waiting for his response.

Hearing no answer, the pilot began again. "You know, they *eat* dogs here, so it ain't safe for Lucy. But back in the States . . ."

The mention of Lucy on someone's dinner plate increased his nausea, so Max sucked in the air and let it out slowly through his nostrils.

When the pilot could wait no longer, he asked, "Uh, how's about if I work for *free*?"

Max gripped his belt and looked past the duct tape at the clouds. "I don't know," he said, closing his eyes. His voice was weak, but a few confused words escaped his pale lips. "We just lost our butler," he mumbled, "and the chauffeur."

The man spat cheerfully on the floor. "Then it's a deal!"

Max gasped at the realization of what he had said. He quickly added, "I only meant we're a little short-handed. I don't even know your name."

"Beverley Gorman at your service!" chortled the pilot. "Beverley's a family name," he added. "I drive real good. And if you need a butler, I can buttle and do stuff like that." Lucy wagged her tail.

Max mumbled through clenched teeth. "I'd need references," he moaned.

Beverley Ignatz Gorman hummed and rolled up his sleeve to display the tattoo of a dancing girl on his bicep.

Max lost control of his nausea.

CHAPTER TWO

You Watermelon

Max had thought the stink of the plane would never fade from his memory. But the mere sight of Mimi suddenly made the harrowing flight worthwhile. Her eager face was brimming with expectant joy as she awaited his arrival in Montego Bay.

Now they lay on the beach breathing the soft sea air. Calypso music drifted in and out as the waves broke gently on the shore. Mimi adjusted her broad-brimmed hat and moved her beach towel to the shade. In her graceful movements, Max sensed her awareness of his admiration.

For years they had moved through married life in a parallel dance, performing together but never touching. Now they savored a sweet and subtle familiarity with one another. The adventure of discovery sometimes inspired them to reveal private thoughts.

Max looked at the beauty of Mimi's smooth features and remembered the day he asked for her hand in marriage. Her father had given him a terse rejection, and Max felt stung. He was defiant and proclaimed they intended to marry anyway.

"Mimi," he said. "I've been thinking about when I talked to your father. I have a better answer now. I know what I should have said."

She raised her eyebrows expectantly. "What is it?"

Max suppressed a smile. "How about this: He says, 'You *can't* elope!' and I say, 'You watermelon!'"

They laughed together in spurts, dozed and laughed again, until Mimi remembered something. "Do you know what happened Saturday?" she said. "Hetty interviewed Katrinka on the radio."

"Hmm . . . Sorry we missed it," he said. "I hope the audience didn't turn ugly about animal testing. But Hetty knows how to turn it around. Whatever happened, Katrinka's always good for business."

"She probably mentioned her father," said Mimi. "She misses Phil terribly. We all do, but it's a shame she's still mourning over both Phil and Morgan. I wonder if her husband feels it."

"I hope not," said Max. "Joseph's a fine man. And I'm impressed with his plans for the elephant sanctuary."

"It's odd that Katrinka doesn't take his name," said Mimi. "I suppose she wants to keep Phil's."

She sighed with contentment and put her hand in his. "I've been thinking, Max. Let's not hire anyone to replace Swenson. We can manage without a chauffeur, and I'll find someone from outside to come clean the house. That way we'll have the place to ourselves."

Max frowned and stared at the waves. "I have a confession," he said.

Mimi knew to hold her tongue and wait.

The Understanding

A few days later, Katrinka stood at the window of her kitchen and leaned on the marble counter. She gazed across the manicured gardens at the Morganthal mansion. Its stone chimneys gleamed in the morning sun. It appeared Max and Mimi had returned from Jamaica.

She sighed. The entire estate would have been hers if she'd married Morgan. Instead, here she was in the gatehouse.

She turned toward the living room and stopped before a life-sized oil painting of Max and her father in their clown costumes. They had been best friends from their youth. Max was tall, quiet and reserved. Phil had been a cheerful dwarf with an outgoing manner. The two had performed in whiteface with the Morganthal Circus and were in constant demand in wide-spread communities.

Max had the painting commissioned to hang in the big house, but after Phil died he gave it to the heartbroken Katrinka.

CHAPTER TWO

Returning to the kitchen, Katrinka leaned over a low table and its set of small chairs. Max had ordered them to be specially made for her father so he wouldn't have to dangle his short legs.

Katrinka thought how awkward Joseph always looked when he sat there—like a grownup in a kindergarten class. *That's just too bad*, she thought. *I'll never part with Daddy's things.*

When Phil's health had declined, Max Morganthal housed him here in the elegant and spacious gatehouse. After Phil's death, he invited Katrinka to stay on and vowed he would support her the rest of her life.

It occurred to Katrinka there might be some secret reason behind his generosity. If she could discover what it was, maybe she could use the information to her advantage.

In the hall, she paused before an ornate gold-framed mirror. She was admiring her image when a curious thumping arose outside the front door.

If she had stepped onto the porch any faster, Katrinka's foot might have kicked a small dog in the ear. The friendly animal looked up just in time and wagged the length of its body along with its tail. The cause of the thumping sound was a splint strapped to its front leg.

The owner arrived and crouched protectively over his dog. The instant the man straightened and showed his face, Katrinka screamed. Visibly shaken, she stepped back and gripped the hand railing.

"Ignatz?" she said. Her voice was weak and uncertain.

The man appeared startled as well, but he quickly recovered. "Call me Beverley," he said. "Hey, it's a real sweet deal you got yourself here."

"Ignatz . . ." she stammered.

She had the presence of mind to purse her glossy pink lips with annoyance. "I should have known it was you by the smell," she said. "You can't get away with coming here, you know."

"Ha! That's what you think. Mr. Morganthal don't know me."

"Dear Ignatz, he'll know who you are when I tell him," she whispered. Katrinka's lovely long lashes fanned her cheeks.

Ignatz curled back his lips in a sneer and glared at her. "But you won't be talking! Know why? 'Cause you ain't so squeaky clean yourself. It was your stupid idea—getting me to kidnap their son."

She smiled sweetly, employing her dimples as a means of stalling him. "Well, you're the one who kept Morgan tied up," she said. "And who phoned Max Morganthal for the ransom money? You!"

When she tried to hide the shaking of her hands, Ignatz scoffed. "Yeah," he said, "but it was you what lied—making like I'd be your hero if I done it. All that sweet-talk! How dumb you think I am, anyways? You figured on acting like his rescuer. He was s'posed to fall all over you, thinking you saved his life. Well, you misinterpulated. Turns out Morgan and that Hetty was thicker'n flies."

Katrinka raised her chin. "If I can't have him, why should that scarecrow Hetty?"

Ignatz brightened. "I get it now . . . you lost out on Morgan." He leered at her. "You couldn't snag him, but you *still* want it all! Don't you go blabbing about me, you two-timer! And I ain't saying my lips are sealed."

Beverley Ignatz Gorman and Katrinka Wallace stood on the porch with their eyes locked. They understood one another. Maybe it was safer to keep their mouths shut for now.

That evening, Katrinka was waiting for Joseph at the front door. "Joseph," she purred. He smiled cautiously at the surprise. His wife was seldom there to greet him when he entered.

"Joseph, honey," she said. "You won't believe this! Ignatz is here. He's living with the Morganthals—working for them and doing who knows what."

CHAPTER TWO

Joseph's smile faded, but he raised his eyebrows with interest.

Katrinka took a gasping breath. "He threatened to tell Max and Mimi about, you know, that little fiasco. I know *you* wouldn't tell anybody about it, would you, Joseph?" She held her breath and waited for an answer.

"It's your place to do that, not mine," he said. "Don't you think you'd better level with them right away?"

"Oh, you don't understand," she said. "I could never tell them! You've always known me inside and out, no matter what. But it isn't that way with Max and Mimi."

"I do understand," he said. "You think you need to put up a false front for fear they'll ask you to leave this place."

"Oh, Joseph! Joseph . . . you *know* that's not all. I couldn't stand to have Morgan think badly of me. Not after I've cared about his opinion all my life."

"I appreciate your honesty, Trink."

She chose not to notice the sorrow in his eyes and continued speaking. "Even if Hetty suspects I was behind the kidnapping, she won't talk. Miss-Goody-Two-Shoes never says anything negative about anybody."

"That might seem like a flaw to you," he said, "but some of us think it's a virtue."

Joseph sat briefly in one of Phil's short chairs, perhaps to avoid facing Katrinka's annoyance. He stood again, remembering she thought he looked ridiculously tall sitting there.

After a sweet little sigh, Katrinka said, "All those years Max and Mimi were drinking and partying," she said, "Daddy practically raised Morgan. You can't imagine how lonely he must have been with me away at boarding school.

Joseph knew the loss of her father was painful for his wife, and he used it as an excuse to put his arm around her tiny waist.

He glanced at the stove. There was nothing cooking. "I'll take you out to dinner," he said.

Katrinka already held his car keys gracefully in her manicured hand. "As long as we're not eating at your sister's. Marian's cooking would have poisoned us by now, if it wasn't for Leaf."

She looked at her image in the mirror and smiled wistfully. Perhaps she was still thinking of her father Phil and the wealthy Morgan. Would they continue to be the only important men in her life?

Joseph took the keys from her dainty fingers. "I hope you'll always be truthful with me, Trink. I need to know I can count on that, at least."

Katrinka laughed and powdered her nose. "Of course," she said. "Honestly, Joseph! What choice do I have, the way you read my mind?" Raising her chin, she adjusted a few curls with her perfect pink fingernails.

"Your honesty comes at a price," he said. "You used to flirt with me for an invitation to dinner."

Freydis Returns

Today was the day Freydis would arrive. Within the hour Leaf would bring her to the cottage.

Morgan had brought the dresser and the four-poster bed down from the attic. The white linen sheets smelled fresh from drying in the sunshine. Hetty had ironed them with special attention to the broad border of lace. When they looked smooth and tight over the puffy mattress cover, she folded the lace edge crisply over the quilt she and her mother Dora had made.

She fluffed the feather pillows and smoothed on the counterpane. "I couldn't have asked for a kinder headmistress than Aunt Freydis. I had no idea she was my aunt—or that she and Father Leaf were watching over me in a special way.

CHAPTER TWO

Morgan put the drawers in the dresser. "It was a miracle you discovered each other," he said. "When your house was destroyed, did you sleep here in the sunroom?"

Hetty sat on the edge of the bed. "Yes. After the tornado, Aunt Freydis and Father were wonderful. They made the three of us feel completely at home. It was a magical time, really. Of course I will always be a Lawrence, but that's when it suddenly became clear I was a Locke as well. Father and Papa seemed like they'd never been apart," she said.

"Well," said Morgan, "it was their ties to you that brought them close again. It's a wonder Leaf ever recovered after your mother died. I'm sure it's because he trusted Dan and Dora so completely."

"Yes, but I was a lot of work, with my heart trouble. And before my operation—all those years of home schooling."

Hetty looked around her at the sunlight that poured through the cottage. "None of us cared how long it took to rebuild our house," she said. "We could have stayed here with them forever."

She looked through the archway at the piano. "I loved my violin lessons with Father. And piano with Aunt Freydis."

She sighed. "I never expected to put music on hold. It's not that I'm good at the violin or ... or anything. I just *wanted* to be. I don't know what happened." Her eyes were downcast, and her fingers felt for the lace handkerchief in her pocket.

"I suppose *I'm* what happened," said Morgan. "I'm sorry."

"Oh, no! I'll *never* be sorry about you! You and Pippa. It's just that I still want to do so many things. And they all take time away from everything else." A tear rolled down her cheek. "And I don't know what Aunt Freydis will want to do all day."

Morgan walked around to where she sat. "I wish I could help you," he said. He pressed her head against his chest and stroked her soft hair. "You're the only one who can decide what to give up."

She looked up at the kindness of Morgan's dark blue eyes then slowly rose to face him. "I don't plan to give up anything," she said.

Though she stood slightly taller than his six feet, Hetty's height had never been significant to Morgan. At this moment, however, it added emphasis to her determination.

Morgan took both her hands. "Changes are coming," he said. "Maybe you're trying to take on too much. No one can be all things to all people."

A cry for help welled up inside her, but Hetty was able to hide it behind a brave smile. "But *you* are, Morgan." Hetty moved toward his embrace; however, the phone rang, and he went to answer it.

Pippa crawled out from under the bed and tugged on her mother's skirt. "I'm hungry," she said. "I want pasketti."

"You want spaghetti, honey?"

Morgan's hand rested on the phone, but he let it ring again and winked at Hetty. "She means gaspetti."

Pippa tried a second time. "Umm . . . skabetti."

Morgan answered the third ring and glanced at Hetty. "Yes, Katrinka, she's here. Just a minute." Hetty stiffened her spine.

At that moment, the gravel driveway crunched under her father's car. Katrinka would have to wait. Leaf had arrived with Freydis.

Hamlet to the Rescue

Max clenched his teeth and paced absently around the study.

Mimi inserted a leather bookmark in the play she was reading. "It's about Beverley, isn't it? You explained it was all a big mistake. I can understand how it happened."

"I don't know what to do with him," said Max.

Mimi shook her head. "I don't either. Unfortunately, when I send him out for an errand, he always comes back."

CHAPTER TWO

"All I care about is the dog," said Max, "otherwise I'd send the lout back to Jamaica. He knows I've done all I can—the vet can't help. Maybe he feels some obligation. He's polishing the paint off the cars."

"Not the Duesenberg, I hope."

"No, just the Cadillacs. He knows the Rolls and the Duesey are off-limits."

Mimi was relieved. She had recently taken an interest in her husband's car collection.

"All Beverley talks about is movies," said Mimi. "He says before he had Lucy, he used to sit through westerns and gangster movies all day. He even memorized them. Have you heard him imitate John Wayne?"

"No, but I've seen him pick his teeth," said Max. "I wonder, Mimi—Don't you have the reel of *Hamlet?* I could put it on the movie projector."

"That's a thought, but Sir Laurence Olivier is a big change from John Wayne."

At first Beverley answered their suggestion with moderate suspicion. However, the following day, he and Lucy arrived to watch *Hamlet*.

It was evening when they finally emerged from the lower floor. Mimi met Beverley at the top of the stairs to prevent his wandering through the private living quarters.

"Man!" he said, "that Oliver guy, he says scads of words what ain't real. But you know what? He pulls it off real good like as if they was! Leastwise that's what I says to Lucy the second time I seen it." Lucy cocked one ear as if to corroborate his statement.

"Actually," said Mimi, "if you want to see *Hamlet* again, I have a book with exactly what you heard. You could take it downstairs and follow along with the movie."

Beverley's mouth fell open. "You mean there's a book to go with it? That Oliver guy, he's one smart interpenoor. All movie stars oughta do like that, for crying out loud!"

Again the next day, Mimi and Max saw little of Beverley. As before, they met him at the top of the stairs that evening. Max confronted him first. "What's going on down there?" he said. "I can't think you've been watching *Hamlet* all this time."

"I wouldn't have gave up yet," said Beverley, "but the perjecter kinda broke down. All that blood at the end, that's what done it. You know, when they all bump each other off."

Mimi hid her amusement with a handkerchief. "You surprise me," she said, "staying interested so long."

Beverley struck a dramatic pose. "Methinks the time is out of joint," he replied. Lucy looked up at him adoringly. "Say, 'methinks' ain't a actual word, is it?"

"It is," said Mimi. "But Shakespeare did invent a lot of words."

"Huh? Like what?"

Mimi thought briefly. "Well," she said, "there was no such word as 'bloodstained' before he wrote *Titus Andronicus*. Another one is 'eyeball.'"

"That ain't no big deal," said Beverley. "Even *me, I* could've told him we gotta have them two words."

He took Lucy outside briefly then headed for his living quarters for the night. As he entered, he sniffed his underarms. *Methinks I gotta take a shower again this week, like that dame Katrinka says.*

Meanwhile, Max and Mimi climbed the back staircase nursing a sense of urgency. The broken projector meant they had to think of some way to occupy Beverley's time, or he might be underfoot all the next day. Mimi had an idea. "Let's send him over to help Hetty," she said.

In no time she had her daughter-in-law on the phone. "Hetty, would it help if our new man took your Aunt Freydis for a drive? Maybe even tomorrow?"

"Thank you," said Hetty. "But don't you need him?"

"We'll manage."

Max took the phone from his wife. "Truthfully," he said, "we're trying to keep him busy."

CHAPTER TWO

"Well," said Hetty, "She could visit her husband's grave."

"Good. We'll send him over in the morning. Freydis can keep him as long as she likes." He slowly hung up the phone.

The next morning, Max and Mimi called Beverley into the sitting room. They didn't invite him to take a seat, but that didn't stop him. He sprawled over the maroon damask settee. Lucy perched on his lap with the delicacy of a born lady. She inclined her shoulder against her beloved Beverley Ignatz Gorman and thumped her tail cheerily against the gold carvings of the armrest, avoiding contact with the fabric.

Max relaxed his scowl and stroked her velvety muzzle, but Mimi's eyes were on Beverley. "You'll be driving a fine lady today," she said. "It's a special opportunity. A privilege. We want you to be prepared. Freydis—Mrs. Fairburn—was headmistress at Haxton Academy, where our daughter went to school."

"She was like the boss principal?" he asked. "I ain't scared of them types no more."

"That's fine. We want you to enjoy it. We have one suggestion that might help: find a way to avoid saying 'ain't,' if you can."

Max joined her. "Or don't talk at all," he said. "You won't need to. I'm sure Hetty can give you the necessary instructions."

"Who?" he seemed alarmed at the name. "Uh, do I gotta do this?"

They were not about to let Beverley weasel out of driving. They continued to make suggestions about opening doors and tipping his cap. He chewed on a fingernail as if pretending to listen. When the lecture was over, he and Lucy went out to the limousine.

"And blah, blah, blah," he mumbled, "right, Lucy?" Ignatz pulled down the brim of his uniform cap to hide his face. "I could tell you a thing or two about principals." His sneer told Lucy she wouldn't want to hear what they were.

Mimi laid her head on her husband's shoulder. At last they were alone. "I don't know, Max. Should we feel guilty about this?"

His arm slipped around her waist. "Probably," he said.

To the Cemetery

It was almost ten o'clock. Hetty put a shawl around her Aunt Freydis's shoulders. "Max and Mimi's chauffeur should be here in a minute or two. I'm sure he'll come to the door for you," she said.

Freydis smiled at Hetty. "Remind me, dear . . . why did we pick the flowers?"

"They're for Uncle John's grave. You'll be going to the cemetery where he's buried."

"Uncle John?"

"Yes . . . I mean your husband, John." Hetty held back the curtains to look out front. "I feel like I know him, because he made all the legal arrangements for Mother and Papa to adopt me."

Bewildered, Freydis blinked her soft gray eyes. "Am I your mother?" she asked.

"You're my wonderful Aunt Freydis." Hetty adjusted the shawl. "When we first met, you were my headmistress at Haxton Academy."

Freydis smiled. "Yes, and you called me Mrs. Fairburn, but I knew who you were. You looked just like your mother," she said. "Henrietta Anne died, didn't she?"

A squeal from the loft upstairs indicated Pippa was not asleep. Hetty looked up the staircase and said, "Maybe a hot water bottle will help her earache."

Freydis pulled on her white gloves. "I'll wait out by the gate. What is his name, dear?"

"I don't know. I'd like to go with you and meet him."

Before Hetty could find the hot water bottle, Freydis raised the wrought iron latch and slipped out the front door. She crossed the little steppingstones and passed through the trellis laden with pink roses. A gleaming black limousine stopped. Its shiny door opened, and she disappeared inside.

When Hetty looked out the window, all that remained of Aunt Freydis was the dust hovering over the gravel driveway.

CHAPTER THREE

Nobody Will Know

Soon after Freydis left in the limousine, Hetty's dear friend and stepmother Marian arrived. She had offered to stay at the cottage with Pippa so Hetty could go to the office for an appointment. She would also be able to greet Freydis on her return.

"I wouldn't impose on you," said Hetty, "but sometimes a professional setting is important."

Marian nodded. "Leaf and I would do anything for you," she said. "Is this client somebody special?" Marian was quick to reverse herself. "Sorry," she said, "I didn't mean to pry. I just know you prefer to work at home whenever you can.

Hetty smiled. "Yes, I do," she said, "and I'll be home as soon as possible. Thank you for being wonderful!"

Marian had a last-minute question. "When Freydis gets back, is there anything I should know?"

"Not really. You'll love seeing how sweet she is with Pippa, but she's not always sure what their relationship is. She may forget you're married to Father," said Hetty. "And sometimes she thinks I'm her daughter."

"Well," said Marian, "It's probably wishful thinking on her part. I'm glad *I* can make that claim." She gave Hetty an affectionate squeeze, and they said goodbye.

Soon Hetty arrived at the office. Throughout her childhood, she had admired the gold and black letters in her papa's office window. They used to spell out *Daniel Lawrence, Attorney at Law*. Now that Hetty and Morgan were his partners, it read *Lawrence, Morganthal & Morganthal*.

She turned the heavy brass doorknob and stepped into a waiting room that seemed unchanged since her childhood. The scent of old books with leather covers gave a comfortable assurance of permanence. Hetty loved the smell of lemon oil with which her mother Dora polished the solid oak furniture.

Fond memories flooded over her. Dora's chocolate chip cookies were on the familiar china plate with blue forget-me-nots around the rim. They were there to welcome all who entered.

Dora Lawrence was standing on a stool, dusting the bookcases. She stopped her work to blow Hetty a kiss. Dora had been Papa Dan's secretary ever since their sickly adopted daughter was well enough to attend school. But Hetty didn't recover from her heart operation until the age of twelve.

The door to Morgan's office was closed. "Is his father in there with him?" asked Hetty.

"Yes. Max just recently arrived," said her mother. Dora tucked a wisp of hair under the braid that failed to contain it. "And I'm sorry your papa's busy too," she said. Dan was on the phone, but he heard them talking and winked at his daughter through the open door.

A flutter of pink femininity flashed outside the window, and soon Katrinka entered in a cloud of perfume. She embraced Hetty and Dora stiffly, but seemed uninterested in casual conversation. She swished past the cookies, preferring to find a seat in Hetty's office immediately.

CHAPTER THREE

"As you know," she said, "I wanted to have this conversation before now."

"Yes," said Hetty. "I'm sorry. My Aunt Freydis was just arriving when you called. At the moment, she's on a drive with Max and Mimi's new chauffeur."

Katrinka's head jerked up, and an artificial smile soon glistened on her pink lips. "Oh, so they have a new man, do they?" She was able to sound exceptionally bored. "Have you seen him?"

When Hetty said she had not, Katrinka attempted to disguise her relief. She frowned and quickly launched into the purpose of her visit. "I think I'll *scream* if I get one more complaint!" she said. "People with allergies . . . they have the gall to blame *me* when their face swells up like a balloon!" To emphasize the sincerity of her emotional outburst, she rolled her lovely big eyes.

Soon she signaled her control with a sweet smile. "I've made a business decision," she proclaimed. "I want to make LuvCon the worldwide star of all the Morganthal businesses. So I'm going to resume animal testing on my entire line of LuvCon products."

"I see," said Hetty. "A few years ago, you felt strongly about ending the practice."

"True," said Katrinka, "but that was then and this is now. Of course, the testing was in place long before *I* came," she said. "You'll remember, in my first press release, I made it clear I'm *against* animal testing, which I am. Truly I am.

"And as you can see, I've set the perfect stage for the public to assume I'm *not* doing it. I want to leave them with that impression. I figure we can sort of slip back into doing it again, later. It's such a totally obvious opportunity, it would be foolish not to take advantage of it."

Her lips formed a righteous little heart shape, and she placed her hands together as if in prayer. "Surely you can see it's for the greater good. And you know I would never do anything *really* wrong. My daddy wouldn't stand for it."

Hetty spread her hands on the ink blotter. "You make a good point, Katrinka. In fact you might ask yourself, 'What *would* my father do?'"

Katrinka tossed her hair and glared at Hetty. "It's not fair to discuss the opinions of someone who's dead."

Hetty leaned forward and began again. "But in a way, he's not. At least he's not dead as long as you keep his memory alive. He loved you, and I know you'll want to make him proud.

After a silent interval, Katrinka fixed her eyes on Hetty. Her father had hoped she and Hetty would be friends. Perhaps she saw the sincerity of Hetty's concern. Her expression softened. Maybe she was puzzled by Hetty's gentle kindness.

She took a long slow breath. "I can close my eyes and picture Daddy." She spoke with sadness. "If only he hadn't sent me away to boarding school." Her eyes took on a distant look, as if searching the past for answers.

Recovering her composure, she said, "You're my lawyer, not my conscience. You're supposed to help me make it work, not stifle my progress." Her chin went up defiantly.

Hetty spoke slowly. "I do want to help you. We can prepare for a press conference explaining your reasons for animal testing. You could conduct a tour of the laboratory at the same time. That way the protestors will see the practice can be humane."

She swiveled in her chair and pulled a book from the shelf behind her. "Russell and Burch—according to them, humane science is the best science anyway," she said. "But just be aware . . . even with following their guidelines, it can mean trading one headache for another."

She waited for a reply.

Katrinka sighed with a tolerance bordering on exasperation. "You really don't understand, do you, Hetty dear? Surely you can see I don't have any choice." She smiled to employ her most adorable dimples. "We can keep it between us," she added with a confidential friendliness. "Nobody else will know."

"You and I would," said Hetty. The blue of her eyes reflected the strength of her determination. "I see two choices and I'm happy to help you with whichever one you prefer. You could either do what you say . . . or say what you're doing."

A frown darkened Katrinka's eyes. "I can't believe you would want people to develop rashes and balloon faces!"

She stormed out with a dramatic flair, a little pout on her glossy pink lips. But her perfume lingered on. "She still wears Bellodgia by Caron," said Dora, opening a window. Hetty washed her face and hands to remove the scent. Otherwise, everyone downwind would know who her client was.

Dora wrapped some cookies in a napkin for Hetty to take home to Pippa. Morgan was still in his office with Max, and the door was closed. Disappointed, Hetty left without seeing him.

Torn

In his usual manner, Max was direct with Morgan—even blunt. But his gaze had none of the hostility Morgan had experienced in the past. "We've talked about forming a clown act," he said. "I want a contract. Spell it all out so we both know what to expect of each other. Family needs these things in writing same as anybody else."

Morgan nodded in agreement.

Max shifted in his chair and kept his eyes on his son. "Don't put me off," he said. "You're not Phil, but you're good." This was a compliment to remember.

Morgan said, "I'll think about it and get back to you." He was quick to add, "It'll be soon, Dad." Experience had taught him to respond to the snap of his father's fingers. He followed

Max into the waiting room and shook his hand at the door. Now he had a decision to make.

When Dan's door opened, Morgan's feet carried him into his office. He didn't need an invitation to sit down with his father-in-law; a comforting blend of respect and familiarity welcomed him. Morgan flashed a grateful smile. "You always know when to be available."

A lopsided stack of papers teetered on the desk. On top was a platter of cookies, which Dan removed and pushed across the desk. He brushed a few crumbs from his lap onto the floor. "Think you'll do it?" he asked.

"I don't know. I'm torn. You already put up with a lot, the way I spend so much time away from the office."

"Don't let that influence your decision," said Dan. "It's going the way we planned. If you and Hetty hadn't joined with me, I'd still be practicing alone."

Morgan's expression was thoughtful. "You must wonder what Hetty wants me to do. My own feelings aren't even clear to me." He shook his head slowly. "I've told you what happened—what I said to Hetty the first time she was on the air—about how much I wanted her at home. I'll feel like a hypocrite if I form a partnership with my dad. It would take a lot of my time."

Dan's kindly face encouraged Morgan to make a confession. He took a deep breath. "I haven't discussed it with Hetty. I'm not sure how. Though it may not be as complicated as I'm making it."

Dan leaned forward. "Or maybe more so," he said. Both men were accustomed to thinking ahead with the skill of chess players.

"With her heart condition," said Morgan, "Hetty mustn't *ever* give birth again. We nearly lost her. I won't take another chance with her life." A new thought occurred to him. "Do you think that's why she keeps busy?" He nodded in answer to his own question. "I bet that's it. So she won't have time to think about it.

CHAPTER THREE

"I don't want either of us to miss Pippa's growing years by being too busy. She's the only child we'll ever have.

"But I can't look in Hetty's eyes and say it. I couldn't stand to see her sadness."

Dan pulled out a large red handkerchief and honked his nose. "I know it's hard on you too," he said. "You just don't want Hetty to know it."

Sorrows were remembered but not mentioned. Hetty's defective heart had made her a frail infant. When Dan and Dora Lawrence adopted her, they were still grieving over the loss of a stillborn son.

Hetty's father Leaf had been married only one short year when his first wife Anne died giving birth to Hetty. He had always known Dan Lawrence would be a wise and kindly father. Though he longed to be a part of Hetty's childhood, Leaf Locke thought it best to remain unseen.

An amusing thought came to Morgan. "Hetty says it's hereditary in her family not to have children." Dan slapped his knee and laughed with his son-in-law. Suddenly Morgan was serious. "Thank you for Hetty," he said.

Dan Lawrence folded his handkerchief and said, "You'll remember Leaf and I *both* gave her away at your wedding."

"Yes," said Morgan. "I mean you were the right kind of father. The way you taught her, she's all about love." He flashed a smile. "She grew up understanding it."

Morgan thought of his parents, Max and Mimi Morganthal, and about the many unhappy years of their marriage. "Right from the start," he said, "Hetty cared about Mom and Dad. For more than twenty years, they never bothered to get acquainted. Then Hetty got Dad to serenade my mother. That anniversary changed everything. Hetty helped them see the best in each other."

Morgan's dark blue eyes were steady. "My dad and I are friends now," he said. "All because Hetty made it happen. For the first time he needs me, and I want to keep our friendship in good repair. I can't put my finger on how she does it.

"So, about my partnership decision—it would be time-consuming. But I know Hetty would be grateful to see how well her efforts have paid off. That's why I'm torn."

A Stunning Day

After her irritating meeting with Hetty, Katrinka hurried to a fashion show downtown and took her place at the head table. Everyone there would be delighted to report they had caught a glimpse of her. As a celebrity behind a well-known face, Katrinka would even be invited to say a few words.

All the models wore LuvCon cosmetics, and the fashions were supplied by a fine women's wear shop in New York City. In attendance was a curmudgeonly woman who was allergic to the adhesive in LuvCon's false eyelashes. She noisily referred to the company as "ScamCon" and was quite public about her search for another brand.

But Katrinka successfully appeased the woman. In a hushed voice, she said, "Let me personally pay your medical bills. Would you be a darling and not mention your little LuvCon experience? Just between us, I've made *incredible* plans to correct the problem!"

There were several superfluous hairs sprouting from the woman's chin. Katrinka tactfully resisted suggesting that before purchasing lashes, or any other additional hairs, she might pluck the ones she already had.

During the drive home, she delighted in recalling the jealousy of the models. She overheard a tall peevish girl named Sabrina, who said, "Why should Katrinka Wallace get all the attention!"

All in all, it was a stunning day. Katrinka was in the spotlight because she represented LuvCon with such grace and style. She could look back on her accomplishments with satisfaction. The only disappointment of the day had been her irritating meeting with Hetty that morning.

CHAPTER THREE   61

I need her on my side, she mused, *because everyone believes Hetty.*

When the wall surrounding the Morganthal estate came into view, Katrinka was nearly home. At the guardhouse, she slowed her car and winked at the young man on duty. It always amused her to see how flustered he was when she approached. With a respectful salute, he blushed and opened the gate to admit her.

Joseph's car was already home at the gatehouse. Katrinka stared at it and pulled in behind the boxwood bushes so he couldn't see her from the kitchen window. She remained at the steering wheel and rested her head against the window to gather her thoughts.

Hetty won't tell anyone about the animal testing. She can be trusted to keep things to herself. I wonder if that's why Daddy wanted us to be friends.

But if I go ahead with my plans, she'll probably talk me out of it. I just know she'll make me change my mind. It's not right. She's a little too honest, if you ask me. I don't like the way she makes me wonder if I'm wrong.

I could tell exactly what she was thinking. She thought it so loud I could hear her brain. As if I need my lawyer to be my conscience or something! Was it some trick?

No, I suppose it was in my own head. But why is she always right? She's annoyingly pleasant about it. Is that why people trust her? I wish they didn't.

Why should I care? I'm successful. I was born beautiful. My looks open doors. Hetty Lawrence will always be a tall, shapeless scarecrow with too much hair. A nobody.

Suddenly, for reasons she didn't understand, Katrinka wanted to be with Joseph. She sat up tall to catch a glimpse of him in the window, but he wasn't visible through the boxwoods. She ran her fingers lightly over her face. Perhaps it wasn't as firm and smooth as she thought.

It seemed fine. And in the soft light, any wrinkles were probably invisible. She smiled.

What am I thinking? I don't have to impress my husband . . . or look pretty for him. He doesn't even care when I take off my eyelashes at night. Joseph loves me anyway, as long as I'm honest with him. And he trusts me.

He's like a pair of comfortable house slippers. Maybe I haven't appreciated him enough. Daddy was right to say he'd make me happy.

A contented smile was on her pink lips. She breathed deeply with a lighthearted joy. Even Hetty's unreasonable attitude could no longer dampen the successes of the day. As she hurried up the front steps to Joseph, Katrinka was almost giddy with anticipation.

Protecting LuvCon

When Katrinka opened the front door, she wanted to see Joseph. She was not disappointed. He knew the sound of her pink high-heeled shoes and was waiting with his hand on the doorknob.

Her kiss was light so she wouldn't smear her lipstick. They laughed, because what did it matter how she looked? The workday was over. He appeared poised to make another go at it, but she made it known that would be all for now.

"I presume you've had a good day?" he asked.

"The best!"

He lifted her off her feet. "Tell me about it. You met with Hetty, didn't you?"

Katrinka said nothing.

He tried again. "How is she?"

"Why do you care?"

"I care because you met with her. I'm interested in everything about you."

CHAPTER THREE

"Well, it was a business meeting."

He waited and watched her face. "I think Hetty could be a good friend, Trink."

"You and Daddy!" She worked the dimples in her pink cheeks just for him. "You won't start that again, will you?" she asked.

He laughed. "No indeed. We'll talk about whatever you like."

"Well," she sighed, "it won't be Hetty Morganthal."

She kissed him again, this time with less regard for her lipstick. Perhaps that would stop his line of questioning.

She blinked sweetly, and Joseph looked at her with obvious curiosity.

"Ooh," she said, "are you trying to learn company secrets?"

He grinned with amusement. "We're on the same team, Trink," he said. "I protect elephants and you protect faces."

She flipped back her hair to show she was ready to move on. "You just looked worried or something," she said.

"No, not at all. I trust Hetty to give you good advice."

"But without Hetty's advice, you still trust me, don't you?"

"You know I do. But if Hetty's involved, so much the better."

Katrinka pursed her lips. Joseph seemed to sense there was something she wasn't telling him. He had more to say. "I have a good working relationship with Morgan," he said. "I was just hoping it could be the same with our wives.

She tilted her head. "You feel like you and Morgan are friends?"

"Of course."

If Katrinka was ready to inquire about Morgan, she was tactful enough to avoid the subject. By the time she put her purse away and removed her shoes, she appeared ready to share what had been on her mind earlier.

Joseph wore a sympathetic expression and waited for her on the couch.

Instead of sitting next to her husband, Katrinka perched daintily on his lap—perhaps to avoid looking into his eyes. "Honeybun," she said, "Hetty made me promise not to say anything. So you can't tell Morgan I told you."

Joseph frowned. "I'm not fond of secrets, Trink. You know that."

"Oh, Joseph, it's just that I need to confide in you because it's so awful. I really don't have anywhere else to turn." She nestled her head into his neck and sniffed. Joseph's frown softened somewhat. She gained control over her emotions and continued.

"And I should probably tell you about this before Hetty does something worse."

Joseph's frown returned. "Whatever it is," he said, "I'm sure there's some misunderstanding."

Katrinka's eyes were moist, and she let Joseph see them for a moment. "It's not that simple. After all I've done to build LuvCon," she whispered, "I'm so afraid the news will leak out and damage the company."

He raised his eyebrows.

She covered her face with her hands. "Hetty's making me do animal testing. I didn't want to do it." Suddenly a little sob came from somewhere, and Katrinka put her fingertips to her throat. "Worst of all, she's pressuring me to deny it. I know she'll blame it on *me* if I say anything at all!"

Standing so Joseph could appreciate her graceful curves, she spoke softly. "I don't think you should tell Morgan. Even with you being good friends."

After a short pause she gasped. "I just realized something— You'll both want to protect LuvCon! But you won't tell Morgan I said anything, will you?"

Joseph stood. "I'll see for myself," he said. There was weariness in his movements. "I've got a key. Is the lab under your building where it was before?"

CHAPTER THREE

Soon he would see the laboratory with all the little caged animals, and Morgan would join him in condemning Hetty's deception. Katrinka turned to conceal a little smile.

Joseph's face took on an unfamiliar sadness, and he was gone.

Katrinka watched from the window as Joseph's car disappeared from view. She tried to sort through her complicated uneasiness.

He was so kind . . . so tender. I need him more than I realized. Daddy knew it all along. It was better than I expected, the way he comforted me. He trusts me and believes what I said. Joseph loves me for my honesty. It's what we have together.

That scarecrow, Hetty—Why did he have to mention her name and spoil everything? Why does he trust her?

He won't anymore, the way I fixed it.

She wondered if the couch could still be warm. It was, and she sat where Joseph had been moments earlier. Closing her eyes, she smiled and rocked back and forth, pretending he still cradled her on his lap.

Suddenly she realized what would happen, and her motion stopped. *He trusted me! What have I done? Joseph . . . my Joseph.* His warmth was not enough to prevent her tears from flowing.

When he returned an hour later, Katrinka was lying on the couch in the dark. He listened to her breathing. She was only pretending to sleep. As if waiting to see him, she wore her prettiest soft, pink nightgown.

Joseph went into the back bathroom and brushed his teeth for a very long time. The foam took even longer to swirl down the drain. He spat in the washbasin again and watched until the water disappeared.

Slowly, he went to his closet and put away his shoes. He couldn't help seeing the dress Katrinka wore earlier. It was now draped suggestively against his suit. He moved it to her side of the closet. Returning to the front room, he stood across from her. The moonlight shone on her face, and there were tears on her cheeks.

"Joseph," she said, "There's something I should tell you." She was crying softly.

Her words were slow in coming, so Joseph said, "I saw the lab."

"You didn't show Morgan, did you?"

"Yes, I did." He sounded stern.

She turned her face away, and her shoulders shook with sobs.

"You have something to tell me, don't you, Katrinka?"

"No . . . not really," she said. Her voice was faint.

"I love you, Joseph."

Nuts

Freydis wore her periwinkle blue hat in anticipation of another morning drive. Stepping with care along the path, she passed under the arbor of climbing roses and looked back toward the cottage.

Hetty stood in the window and waved. The room behind her was bathed in sunlight. The soft puffs of her hair seemed to capture the beams and illuminate the surrounding space.

Pippa stood on a tufted seat next to her mother and pressed her nose against the windowpane. Fresh from the bathtub, water dripped from her tangled curls. When the child had finished blowing kisses to her great aunt Freydis, Hetty wrapped the towel snugly around her shoulders and held her close.

Freydis steadied herself against the gate and waved to them with a white-gloved hand. Before she had time to sit on the bench, Max and Mimi's shiny black limousine arrived. The driver pulled his cap down to shade his eyes and came to her aid from the other side.

CHAPTER THREE

"Please, young man," said Freydis, "remind me of your name."

"It's Beverley. Beverley Gorman," he said. "So, where to?" He helped her into the back seat.

"I beg your pardon, Mr. Gorman?"

"I said, where you want to go, lady? It don't matter none to me and Lucy."

"Lucy? Is she your wife?"

"Nope. My dog."

"Your daughter, you say?"

Ignatz spoke louder. "My dog! You seen her when you got in. Last time, too."

"Oh, yes. A nice little dog." She laughed as if to apologize. "My husband has a dog. It even likes to hear him play the violin."

"But your husband's dead. You couldn't find his grave, but we looked for it, remember?"

She looked out the window until it came to her. "Yes, that's right. My brother is the violinist," she said. "He taught Hetty. Do you know my Hetty?"

"Huh? I ain't no expert on who's who, but Hetty ain't yours, lady."

"I'm so sorry, Mr. Gorman, but I'm having difficulty hearing you."

He rolled his eyes. "I think you're nuts, lady."

She smiled. "I think you're nice too, Mr. Gorman."

He slowed the car and turned to glance at her.

It was quieter now, so he spoke again. "You gotta 'scuse my grammar, Mrs. Fairburn, ma'am. Morganthals tell me I ain't s'posed to say ain't. But there ain't nothing else as good, when that's what I mean."

Lucy put her head in his lap.

Freydis smiled with her eyes. They were soft and kind. "In France," she said, "everyone uses double negatives."

"No lie? Double negatives, you say." He sat a little taller. "I'm like talking French. That where you been living?"

"Not far from there. I was in England."

The brakes screeched, and the car pulled over to the side of the road.

"Let me tell you, something," said Ignatz. "There's this guy Shakespeare, see. He's the main thing what England's about, if you ask me!"

Freydis Fairburn blinked her large gray eyes and leaned forward. "If you don't mind, Mr. Gorman," she said, "I might hear you better if I were to join you in the front seat."

Squeezing Out the Answer

Katrinka stood in her front window gazing across the expansive lawns and gardens of the Morganthal estate. When she saw Ignatz depart in the Morganthals' limousine, she knew the time was right. She could talk to Max now about the question that occupied her mind.

Checking her image in the mirror, she turned her head a little. If she should happen to see Max, the right side of her face might be the one to put forward. She was proud of the slightly more humble appearance of the other side, but perhaps the confident look of her right side would be best. With just a little powder to touch up her nose, she was ready.

To be fully prepared, Katrinka rehearsed the conversation she hoped would take place. It was important to seem casual. Maybe she could talk of the weather first and then say, in a rather offhand way, "Oh, something just occurred to me . . . " Then she could launch into the trickier matter.

Such were Katrinka's thoughts as she crossed the manicured lawn toward the big house. But her plans proved unnecessary when Max suddenly emerged from the boxwood garden. He surprised her with a greeting. This was the best possible situation. They laughed a little and spoke of nature's beauty. Katrinka was able to make a seamless transition from that into the topic of her choice.

CHAPTER THREE

"Oh, Max, I'm the luckiest person alive . . . and not just because I get to see you and Mimi so much!" Her long lashes fanned her rosy cheeks. "I have to pinch myself, it's so beautiful here. Sometimes I wonder how this could have happened to little me." She cocked her head and smiled wistfully.

Max said nothing. Katrinka waited long enough for his response that it was a bit awkward. The corners of her mouth turned up just enough to enliven her dimples, and she began again. "To think I can stay here the rest of my life! It's just too good to be true, Max." She pursed her pink lips sweetly. "I just know you'll tell me why!"

Max gave his blunt answer. "No," he said, "I won't."

Katrinka suspected his answer concealed useful information. She had a gift for knowing what secrets would be to her advantage. "Oh, Max," she cooed, "you're such a tease!"

Ordinarily, Katrinka was not one to back down, but she knew Max had his limits. The set of his jaw expressed a firm resolve.

However, the thought did occur to her that Max might feel apologetic about his refusal. If so, this could be the right time for another question. She turned the left side of her face to him. "There's something else I want to know. You can tell me anything!" she said with a confidential wink. "That's how close I feel to you and Mimi."

Max did appear to be listening, so Katrinka got closer and looked up into his eyes. Her expression was dreamy with hope.

"Max, honey," she said, "Why did you make that financial agreement? You know . . . about Morgan's inheritance? The way he would get everything just if he married me."

More than anything, she needed to hear how much he and Mimi had wanted her for their daughter-in-law. Her eyes pled with him.

The night she had cried herself to sleep, Joseph seemed strangely unmoved. Now she mostly needed to know somebody cared. If nothing else, maybe Max would speak of his admiration for her father. Max and Mimi must have offered that financial incentive so Morgan would choose her instead of Hetty. That could explain why they kept the agreement in place until the last minute.

"Why, Max?" she repeated. "You can tell *me*!" Her lovely eyes were shining as she waited for his explanation.

"You don't want to know," he said.

"I do, Max. Really I do."

He looked away and tried to change the subject. "So . . . you and Joseph like the gatehouse?"

Katrinka was determined to squeeze out his answer. "Max," she said, "I believe you're afraid I'll tell Hetty!" She laughed and put her hands on her hips. "She can take it. She's a big girl."

Max seemed to know Katrinka would keep asking, so he gave her the truth without further delay. "At first it was because of my friendship with your father," he said, "but Phil never liked the idea. He was afraid if Morgan did marry you, it would look like money was the motive. He wanted better for you."

Katrinka smiled and cocked her head with interest. "But after that?" she asked. "I mean, why did you leave it in effect until Morgan and Hetty were married?"

"We thought Morgan would marry Hetty," said Max, "but we had to know it was for the right reasons."

A blush crept across Katrinka's face, and she had to steady herself by looking at the horizon.

Max continued. "Morgan chose Hetty in spite of the agreement. It proved he didn't do it for the money. He was willing to give up his inheritance to marry her."

"Oh, yes . . . yes, of course," said Katrinka. Her lip trembled, and she was unable to maintain her smile. "Whatever makes sense . . . I mean, you know best."

Max may have suspected his answer was hard on her, and he quickly added another explanation. "For Mimi and

CHAPTER THREE

me, money was a curse," he said. "But you know that. People thought I married her out of greed. Even Mimi did. It made for twenty years of a bad marriage. I wasn't about to let the same thing happen to my son."

There was no place Katrinka could rest her eyes to hide her humiliation.

The Outing

Hetty placed a jar of icy lemonade in the bottom of the picnic basket and tightened the lid. Next she added a square container of potato salad and hoped it would prop the jar upright.

"Thank you dear," said Freydis. "John loves potato salad."

"I'm so glad," said Hetty. "Although I'm not so sure the driver's name is John. I know he took you to Uncle John's grave the first time."

"Yes, that's right," said Freydis. She smiled and tried to adjust her hat so the veil would be out of her eyes.

Hetty helped her. "You enjoy these outings, don't you?"

"Yes, I look forward to our visits. He's such a nice young man."

Freydis always ate small portions. In fact Morgan said a hummingbird couldn't do much humming on what she ate. But in case the driver had a manly appetite, Hetty wrapped five generous pieces of fried chicken in foil and tucked them in the basket along with a bag of potato chips.

Pippa flattened two red gingham napkins over the chips. Chewing earnestly on her tongue, she smashed them down nice and smooth with her pudgy fingers.

When the limousine arrived at the gate, Hetty handed Freydis her purse and gloves. "We'll walk out with you," she said.

Oddly, the chauffeur made no move to help Freydis to her seat. Certainly he had seen them coming; however, he remained in place. Hetty opened the rear door for her.

"We can put the basket here," said Freydis, "but I'll be sitting in front."

While Pippa hugged Freydis around the knees, Hetty leaned forward to introduce herself to the driver. She was surprised at the little dog wagging its tail next to him.

The man kept his face hidden behind the shiny black brim of his cap. "Gorman here," he said.

Later that afternoon, Hetty realized she had completely lost track of the time. When Freydis returned to the cottage, she looked frail but happy.

"The lunch was delicious, Hetty dear," she said.

Mr. Gorman stood in the doorway. His dog was on one arm and the picnic basket on the other. Freydis smiled and whispered in his ear. "What was it we ate?"

He spoke up cheerily. "Man, that was some chicken!"

Hetty laughed and embraced Freydis while Mr. Gorman entered. When he had delivered the basket to the kitchen table, he faced Hetty and removed his hat.

"Oh!" she cried. Hetty was unable to muffle her shock, but tried to control her words. "You . . . you surprised me."

In the awkwardness of the moment, they turned and watched Freydis walk into the sunroom.

"Yes, ma'am. It's me, Ignatz." He shifted his weight from one foot to the other, and Lucy licked his ear.

"To tell the truth, ma'am, I been trying to remain synonymous. 'Cause if any of the old circus folks figured out it was me, I reckon there'd be trouble."

He brightened a little and said, "I'm glad you didn't get stomped on like your husband. Where I left you, I swear I didn't know about no elephant in there. Not when I tied you up, anyways."

CHAPTER THREE

Hetty caught her breath. "Thank you, Ignatz. We got your note. I know you came back to make sure I was safe."

"Yeah." He slapped his cap against his thigh.

Ignatz appeared self-conscious, but when Freydis smiled at him from the sunroom, he nodded respectfully and continued.

"Even grandmas like her what don't knit things—they give real terrific advice. On account of being up in years and all. Now, I ain't never had me a grandma, see. And Mrs. Fairburn ain't had no grandkid. But her and me, we just pretend like it anyways.

"Mrs. Fairburn, she says everybody oughta know who people are. You know Shakespeare hisself might be somebody else, in actual fact! There's even folks think he's a guy named Bacon. For crying out loud, he could be bacon and eggs, for all I care, long as the stuff he wrote is all the same. We just wonder by who, right?

"Anyways, me and her, we decipher as how Shakespeare oughta not be synonymous. And that's why Mrs. Fairburn says neither should I."

He shifted his weight. "Now you know how come I told you it's me. Beverley Ignatz Gorman."

Not Squishy

Later that evening, the world seemed at peace. Pippa fell asleep over dinner and went willingly to bed. Freydis was at her desk sorting through old letters. She forgot having read them recently.

In the front yard, Hetty and Morgan lay nestled together, testing the comfort of their new hammock.

"Perfect," said Morgan.

Hetty readjusted her shoulder and put her arm across his chest. Morgan held her hair away from his mouth. "Are you comfortable?" he asked.

"I sort of am," she said. "It's just that you're . . . let me think . . . " She was looking for the right word.

"I'm what?"

"You're not squishy," she said. "I mean not squishy enough for comfort."

He grinned. "I'll try to be squishier," he said.

"If you were a pillow, I could do like this." She laughed and socked his chest.

He howled in mock pain. "I can see the headlines: *Woman Wounds Husband in Revenge for Unsquishiness.*"

Hetty laughed. *"Wife Seeks Damages for Discomfort."*

Morgan made payment in the form of a noisy kiss on her pink cheek. "One smooch," he said, "paid in full."

Hetty had tied back her hair with a blue satin ribbon, but the flyaway puffs tickled his nose. "*Man Chooses Death by Hair,*" he said, smoothing it back. His thumb lingered where Hetty's hair came to a soft peak in the middle of her forehead. She blinked her pale lashes and looked at him with eyes blue as the sky and bright with happiness.

They lay still for a while listening to the evening song of a robin until Hetty sat upright to tie back her hair. "I won't have you suffocating," she said. "Katrinka offered to cut it for me."

He rested his hand on her back. "If you like, but I wasn't complaining. In fact, what a way to go."

Hetty looked beyond the white picket fence at the distant forest. "I had a surprise today, Morgan." She turned to see his face and then looked to the forest again. Already it was darker than when they had put up the hammock. "It's about your parents' new chauffeur, " she said.

He put his hands behind his head. "What is it?"

"Well, you know how good he is to Aunt Freydis. And he takes her wherever she wants."

Morgan waited with interest for Hetty to continue.

"I haven't told your parents about him," she said. "When we first met, he said his name was Gorman. Then he brought Aunt Freydis home. That's when I found out who he is."

"Who is he?" asked Morgan.

"Ignatz."

"Ignatz? You can't mean my kidnapper." He propped himself up on his elbow. "And you didn't tell Dad?"

Hetty didn't respond.

"Why not, Hetty?"

"He's different now," she said. "Couldn't we wait a while? Aunt Freydis is so happy."

Morgan was silent.

Hetty turned to glance at him. "Do you . . . do you think we could give him a chance?"

When at last he spoke, Morgan's voice was husky with disappointment. "You've always been open and forthright. I'm surprised you would keep it from them." He lay back in the hammock.

Hetty stared at a shadowy path at the edge of the wood. It led to the magnificent oak tree, Hannah. She thought of the many years she had found comfort in Hannah's broad branches, but the old oak was dying now and could no longer offer refuge.

Sadness softened Hetty's voice. "People can change," she said. It was almost a question.

Darkness had silenced the birds. Hetty looked toward the cottage. Freydis slept in an overstuffed chair inside the sunroom. A Luna moth, drawn to the light, fluttered against the window.

Morgan slipped his arm around Hetty's waist. "I wish I could agree, but I think you're wrong. We need to be realistic. Ignatz will take advantage of my parents or Freydis, and we've got to tell them."

"Oh . . . but do you think you could talk with Ignatz first? Maybe you'll see him the way I do."

"Of course. Just for you, I'll confront him in the morning."

Hetty tilted her head. "*Confront* wasn't exactly the word I had in mind."

"Okay. It doesn't matter that he abused the animals. That he kidnapped Katrinka and me and almost had you killed in an elephant pen. I'm going to see if he suddenly deserves sainthood."

He pulled Hetty back against his unsquishy self. "Tomorrow, I'll try to have a conversation with the scoundrel. As you can tell, I have an open mind."

"Thank you," she whispered. The soft night air carried the scent of roses, and he touched her cheek. Their first kiss was not enough. Nor were those that followed. It was some time before they went inside.

Cold Stone Steps

The next afternoon, Freydis went for a drive with Ignatz. Hetty couldn't think of any excuse to keep her home. When Freydis had been gone less than half an hour, Hetty sat in the window and worried.

Ignatz may still be angry that Phil fired him from the circus. I can see why Morgan's afraid he'll want revenge on somebody.

I feel comfortable about my own judgment. Still, I'd rather have Morgan's trust than anything. He feels I deceived his parents. What will he think about my letting Freydis go with Ignatz again? I don't even know if he's talked with him yet.

Hetty wished for Freydis to come home immediately. Or at least before Morgan. But it was not meant to be. When a car came, it was Morgan's. Pippa skipped to the gate, pulling Hetty's hand. When her father raised her in his arms, she planted tiny wet kisses on his cheek.

Hetty stood back and looked through the child's curly hair at the intense happiness on Morgan's face. She could see

CHAPTER THREE 77

it in the tiny flecks of brown that danced in his dark blue eyes: his family was his greatest joy.

Hetty felt deep satisfaction, but also pain. She looked away. If only she could give Morgan the many children he deserved! Adopting could involve long, difficult years. From the beginning, Morgan had assured her he would be happy with no family at all. But Hetty knew his declaration was a bald-faced lie—an attempt to preserve her life.

Morgan's arm went around her, and he pulled her close. His whiskers were always rough by this time of day, so he kissed the side of her neck with great care. He seemed to treasure this daily ritual as if it were new and fresh. They walked along the stone path, careful not to tread on the clusters of violets.

A little family of sparrows had set up housekeeping in the ivy surrounding the cottage door, and they now darted around the nest with no fear of being disturbed. Morgan and Pippa had taken a special interest in the blue speckled eggs, which had hatched twelve days after they appeared.

"I'm sorry," said Morgan, "but I didn't have time to go see Ignatz. "Was Freydis okay with staying home?"

"Well, I was . . . I was hoping she would get home before you. So you could see everything is all right."

Morgan stopped where he was. "You can't mean Ignatz took her."

Hetty nodded. No excuses came to her.

Morgan frowned and looked away. "I'm sure she'll be fine," he said. But then came his true feelings. "Ignatz could hold her for ransom. She'd be an easy target." He pulled the car keys from his pocket. "I've got to find them."

When Morgan's car had pulled away, Hetty sat on the cold stone steps and watched the dust dissipate.

Pippa was puzzled by her father's disappearance and looked to her mother for the answer. She watched Hetty's face a moment. "Don't cry, Mommy," she said. "I can make it better." She stooped to pick a violet for her.

CHAPTER FOUR

Trouble

Ignatz rolled his window down and his sleeves up. It was a warm and pleasant afternoon. Perfect for a drive. The trees were in bloom, and the air was heavy with their perfume.

Freydis noticed the tattoo Ignatz had previously hidden under his shirtsleeve.

"Did someone draw on your arm, Mr. Gorman?"

"You could say so, ma'am."

"Oh, now I see . . . it's a lady."

"Huh? Yeah, sure." He rolled his sleeve down to cover it. "I got it on one of my birthdays."

"When *is* your birthday, Mr. Gorman? We must celebrate."

Ignatz placed his hand on Lucy's back, as if to control his own excitement by the act of restraining her. "It was yesterday," he said. "I ain't never . . . I mean I never gone to no birthday party. Not like people do when they got friends. When's yours, Mrs. Fairburn?"

She was not quite sure at first, but then it came to her. "It's not until the middle of August," she said.

He took a minute to count on his fingers, but soon gave up. "I mighta got it figured wrong, but seems like we got us the same day to celebrate!"

"How could that be?" she asked.

"Well, my ma had me the middle of May. That means you started out as a 'bun in the oven,' so to speak, about the same day I was had."

Ignatz wore a broad grin. Now he could go to a birthday party with a real friend.

He suddenly decided to depart from their accustomed route. Before long the limousine stopped just beyond the bakery. Mrs. Fairburn wasn't likely to see him go in there for a birthday cake. He could surprise her.

He told Lucy and Mrs. Fairburn he would be no more than five minutes, but his negotiations took much longer. In the display case, there was only one cake worthy of such an event. Someone had ordered it for an office promotion party. But nobody had picked it up, because the man got fired instead.

The baker agreed to remove the image of a typewriter made of green frosting. He would decorate it with *Happy B day to Me and Mrs. F* instead. The *B* could stand for either *Bun* or *Birth*. There wasn't room for the name *Fairburn*. Ignatz didn't know how to spell it anyway.

The baker was the first to hear something outside. When Ignatz looked through the window, he saw the cause of the commotion and burst out the door. "Forget the cake!" he yelled.

A gang of six ruffians strutted on the sidewalk, taunting Freydis. They jeered and tossed her purse between them over her head. With shaky hands, she groped for her hat underfoot and stumbled when one of them snatched it out of reach.

Ignatz was enraged. His fury left no room for fear, and he stormed toward the gang. "Knock it off, you pernicious morons!"

I never gone to no birthday party.

He glowered at their surprised faces and gathered Freydis in his arms while Lucy barked frantically from the open window.

"You ain't fit to touch the ground she spits on," he said. The group backed off.

Ignatz cradled Freydis against his chest, but his eyes missed nothing, and his voice meant business. His attention was on her hat. Without being told, someone placed it on her head; however, clever hands tried to hide the purse. It had sprung open, and it was unclear whether the contents had scattered.

"Give over," said Ignatz. They were not ready to hand it to him until his next official-sounding threat.

"You want to start a international impudence?" he said. "Me and her ladyship, we'll sic the government on you. Now buzz off!"

His shiny hat and carefully pressed uniform may have helped. For whatever reason, the gang obeyed. They retreated, leaving Ignatz to carry Freydis to the car.

She was shaking. The fall had scraped her knee, and one of her stockings had a run in it. She thanked Ignatz with a weak smile, and he wiped her tears with his tie.

"What marvelous courage," she said. "Dear friend, I'm so very grateful."

Ignatz closed the car door and checked the gutter for any items that might have spilled from her purse. All he found was John Fairburn's pocket watch, which he slipped into the pocket of his jacket.

Ignatz on the Air

The day of the radio show had rolled around again.

Hetty adjusted the microphone and covered it with her hand. "You'll do fine, Ignatz," she said. She smiled with confidence to assure him they would both enjoy the coming interview. "Pretend there's no one listening to us, and you might feel more comfortable. Oh, and the sound of the microphone might surprise you, unless you test it first."

When Ignatz clunked the microphone with his fist, Lucy cocked her head. The table overlapped her customary lap space, so she sat upright and settled her velvety jowls on the tabletop.

The studio audience clapped at a signal from the short bald man who waved the *applause* sign. Ignatz smiled weakly and watched Hetty introduce the show.

"Beverley Ignatz Gorman," she said, "is currently working as a chauffeur for Maximilian Morganthal. He was eager to be on the air today."

Apparently the audience response gave him confidence. "Yeah!" he said, "This show needs a guy what thinks big. Somebody actiony like me, for instance."

When Ignatz heard a sneeze somewhere in the audience, his eyes froze in a stare. Hetty regained his attention with another question. "Tell us what sort of action you like," she said.

"Huh? That's easy." He stroked Lucy. "I got me my own airline company."

"You must like to travel."

"Oh, yeah! That's what I mostly do. See I got me one pilot, and I'm it."

"Where do you like to go?"

"Strictly speaking, I ain't got there yet. But there's this guy I gotta go see. I calls him Ignatz Number One. It's him where I got my name from."

"Why do you want to see Ignatz Number One?"

"Well, years back he writes me. He tells how some senator guy made up this list of communists, and he swears they're all guilty as sin. Ignatz Number One *hisself* was on that list of names, for crying out loud! He begs me to come tell folks how he's a real nice guy and all.

"First off I says, no way! They won't catch me interspersing with no commie, even if he *ain't* one! I'm a real American, see." He folded his arms emphatically.

"Please go on," said Hetty.

"Okay. Anyways, that's how I used to think. Then real unexpected, this gent Morgan Morganthal—who you're conversant with on account of your mutual matrimony—he come to see me. We get talking about, you know, man stuff. And he asks me how did I know Ignatz Number One was a communist? Then I confer as to how it was even in a newspaper, and the guy what wrote up the list was a real big-shot.

"So here's what Morganthal says: If we all decide folks is bad before they been judged fair, the same could happen to anybody. Like for instance *me*! Stuff I done is bad enough, I don't want to be locked up for crud I ain't done."

Ignatz leaned back, apparently satisfied with his public statement.

"I believe you're referring to Senator Joseph McCarthy?" said Hetty. "He did have a lot of people scared."

"Yeah," he snorted. "Maybe he'd of stuck me on the list for saying it, but big-shots can be nincompoops same as anybody!" The audience responded with pleasure at his outburst.

Ignatz continued with more confidence. "Thing is, I been a big-shot consecutive of two different companies. Me and Lucy here, we had us a Whack-a-mole business, too.

Here's what I know: being important is worth pretty near zero—zilch, if you ain't got joy."

He stroked Lucy's ear, and she raised it like a sail before the wind. "Yep," he said. "You gotta have joy. And we gotta do right or it ain't gonna be a pretty picture when we kick the bucket." He scowled to condemn the entire concept of evil. "That's why I gotta find Ignatz Number One and tell him I feel real bereft about what I ain't done for him yet.

"We all end up a bag of bones in the end, see. Somebody can dig up our skull like poor Yorick."

CHAPTER FOUR

Hetty nodded. "You mention poor Yorick, Mr. Gorman . . . That brings up another subject. I understand you're interested in Shakespeare's *Hamlet*."

"Yeah, for sure. Mr. and Mrs. Morganthal, they got this old 35-millimeter movie perjecter they don't hardly use. I expect it's 'cause they go to hoity-toity theaters, instead. You know—singing operas with velvety curtains—and plays on a genuine stage. In them places, they even convolute actors down from the ceiling.

"Mrs. Morganthal, she's a actressy type, and somebody give her a *Hamlet* movie. That's the only reel they got, excepting one of a circus, and that's a homemade one. By some clown friend.

"When I was self-employed—meaning I got no job—I went to the movie theaters and watched flicks all day. We only had to pay one time. Not like now, where you gotta hide out in the men's room with your feet up to keep from getting kicked out. There weren't no books to follow along with. Not like Shakespeare, anyways. But know what? I memorized stuff backwards and forwards. I'm that good. Like the real John Wayne.

"I memorize a ton of *Hamlet*. On the days me and Mrs. Fairburn don't go driving, we just sit and say that stuff together. She thinks I make a terrific Laurence Olivier.

"Anyways, like I say, I got me the pleasure of driving a real great lady! Confidentially," he announced, "I'm talking about your aunt. Just so's everybody knows."

Hetty smiled. "I might add . . . it's a real pleasure for *her*, Mr. Gorman."

He blushed. "Yeah, I know."

Lucy thumped her tail while Ignatz collected his manly self.

Happy Birthday

The day came for Freydis and Ignatz to have the party they had planned. Hetty made them a fried chicken lunch like the one they had praised a few weeks earlier.

This time, Ignatz already had a cake he ordered the day ahead. Mrs. Fairburn's name was spelled out in red sugar letters. It didn't need candles. Freydis wasn't sure how old she was anyway.

"You are my guest of honor, Mr. Gorman."

"What's it like at parties you been to?" he asked.

"I think my last party was with a friend who shared my flat."

"Your flat what?" asked Ignatz.

"That's just what they call an apartment in England."

"If it's got furniture in it, methinks they oughta call it a *lumpy*."

Freydis laughed with pleasure. "That is a very clever idea, Mr. Gorman!"

Lucy looked up at Ignatz as if sensing his joy, and he scratched behind her ears. She wagged her tail and sniffed the air.

"Smells good, don't it, girl?" She cocked one ear and licked her chops at the scent of fried chicken.

Ignatz pulled over where the view was especially beautiful. "Tell you what," he said, "I'll hunt for a spot like the queen of England herself couldn't find none better. I'll be real quick."

Freydis was grateful, and Ignatz saw it in her soft gray eyes. Before now, nobody ever looked at him like he really mattered. He opened the back door and took the padded quilt from the top of the picnic basket.

He crossed a narrow footpath and found a flat area along the gentle slope. A grouping of large flat rocks would serve as tables and seats. Nearby was a tree where he could tie Lucy. He looked at a distant puffy cloud. It looked like Lucy when she was a fat puppy.

Ignatz thought how he wouldn't want to be himself even a year ago. Just now, everything was exactly right.

Mrs. Fairburn, she says Hetty Morganthal once had her a dog. Maybe that's how come she likes everybody, even that two-timing Katrinka. Hetty's real big on forgiving, and stuff like that. She likes me starting over. Even acts like as if I ain't done nothing wrong.

It ain't no secret who I am. Not now. Whether I tell Morganthals or not, what can Katrinka do to me? I wonder about her. Guess she'll get what's coming to her, anyways.

Hetty's ma what borned her, she was named Henrietta Anne same as her. She even talks about her name real proud and all. Like me, it's from a family person what loves her, even if they are dead. She says my ma must have been real proud to have gave me her family name. Yep, that's me—Beverley!

And now I got my Mrs. Fairburn what cares about me a whole lot, too. It's like she's my real grandma, excepting she don't knit stuff and she ain't dead.

He spread the blanket on the ground.

Ignatz liked the responsibility that accompanied being a genuine somebody. He raised his chest and looked toward the limousine.

The Note

Later that afternoon, Max glanced out the window of the morning room and puzzled at what he saw. Why was the limousine in the porte-cochère and not in the garage? He slapped the *Wall Street Journal* against his knee and frowned. Perhaps the tattered note on the windshield was meant to explain it. He hurried down the marble steps and plucked it from under the windshield wiper.

Apparently Ignatz had parked the car there to draw attention to the message. Max sat on the rim of the fishpond and read the note.

> Dear to who it may concern, namely, Mr. and Mrs. Morganthal,
> I got to go away now and I ain't coming back unless if you want me.
> Sincerely,
> Beverley I. Gorman

Max called to ask Hetty what she might know about it.

"Nothing, really," she said. "They went out to have a birthday party. It's been an hour since he brought Aunt Freydis home. We didn't talk. She's fallen asleep in her chair."

"Don't disturb her," said Max. "Not till I figure it out."

Though Hetty agreed to it, something seemed to be terribly wrong. She snatched the car keys and rushed for the door. Freydis could stay resting as she was, and Pippa was with Marian and Leaf.

The guard waved her in through the Morganthals' gate, and Hetty steeled herself to talk to Max. He stood outside the front door. In his hand was the note from Ignatz.

Hetty was pale, but her cheeks were splotchy from distress and feelings of guilt. "There's something I haven't told you, Max."

"It can't be that bad," he said.

Her voice squeaked. "I'm so sorry. I should have mentioned it as soon as I knew."

"Well, what is it?"

"It's about Beverley," she stammered. "He's really the animal trainer, Ignatz."

Max was quiet, and Hetty couldn't raise her eyes to look at him. "He's been kind to Aunt Freydis," she said quietly.

"We may never know the story," he said, "but it looks like there's no harm done. Don't be hard on yourself."

CHAPTER FOUR

After a deep breath, Hetty sounded more like herself. She gave him a smile of relief. "Thank you. You have every reason to be angry with me."

"Not really," he said.

Max glanced at the note. "I wonder why he chose the name Beverley."

Hetty had the answer. "Actually," she said, "Beverley was his mother's maiden name. He went by that until he joined the circus, but he thought the name 'Ignatz' sounded better for an animal trainer."

Max had something else on his mind. He glanced around as if to be sure no one heard him. "I've been keeping something from Mimi, and I'm not sure how to handle it."

Hetty nodded politely and tried to look interested in the topiary bushes. "Whatever it is, Max, I'm sure you can tell her. You mean everything to Mimi. Being open about it can only bring you closer."

Max shook his head. "I can't take that chance. Everything's too good between us now . . ." The angles of his face appeared to soften, and he smiled at Hetty. "You've changed the way we see each other."

"Not really," she said. "You and Mimi did it."

With his hand, Max waved away the untruth of her words. "We're grateful, believe me." He was quiet a moment and then spoke uneasily. "Katrinka's nipping at my heels. She wants to know why I'm letting her live in the gatehouse."

"Your affection for Katrinka and her father is reason enough," said Hetty. "Surely she can see that."

"Well, of course," said Max, "but she thinks there's more to it. And she's right . . . there *is* more. It's something I did to her father. Phil Wallace forgave me, but Katrinka never will."

Hetty looked puzzled.

Max scowled. "If Katrinka learns what it was," he said, "she could tell my wife. My greatest fear is losing Mimi's respect."

He looked away. "I wasn't much of a father, either."

A memory came to Hetty. "Phil told me your influence on Morgan was greater than you know. And you must realize Phil had a strong respect for you. Even more at the end of his life."

"I didn't know that," said Max. He savored Phil's generosity a moment, but soon he scowled. "And I repaid him by wrecking his career," he said, "because I couldn't stand for him to leave."

Normally Max was not given to confessing, but he knew anything he told Hetty in confidence would be well guarded. His daughter-in-law had a kindly respect for privacy and did not need to be reminded to preserve it.

Hetty concentrated on the topiary bushes again. She appeared uncomfortable with hearing further revelations. One bush was trimmed in the shape of a silk top hat. "I'm honored you would confide in me," she said, "but you don't need to."

They spoke quietly for a time. The remorse he expressed only increased Hetty's affection for him.

"Max," she said, "I feel privileged to have the Morganthal name."

Compliments were awkward for Max. He accepted Hetty's kind words by folding and unfolding the tattered note.

She kissed him on the cheek and left for the cottage.

Lucy

Max opened the note from Ignatz and read it again. He crumpled it in his fist and said, "Good riddance."

He spoke aloud but with little conviction. Maybe he had gotten used to the bum. Certainly he admitted to having a real affection for Lucy. In any case, he tightened his lips as if preparing to move on.

CHAPTER FOUR

He was ready to turn back to the house and finish reading the newspaper. That was until he saw the sun reflected from a car window. *Someone must have passed through the entry. Why didn't the guard call ahead? Maybe he did.* Max realized there was no one inside to answer the phone.

Someone's gray Ford crawled toward the house. The driver seemed hesitant to approach, but when at last he pulled in next to Max his car chattered to a stop, and he rolled down his window.

"Excuse me . . . Mr. Morganthal, I believe?"

Max walked toward the driver. "Yes, what is it?"

"Our house is the one between here and what they call 'The Cottage.' Do I have the right place? That is, I mean do you have a chauffeur who carries around a small dog? About so high—a bad leg?"

Max raised his eyebrows to signal he was listening.

The man stepped from his car. "Well, I thought you . . . or somebody might want to know about this."

He went to the rear of the car and opened the trunk for Max to see. There was a pile of gadgets—a crowbar, a jack and several small tools that seemed to have been removed from the adjacent canvas case. Carefully, the man folded back the corners of the canvas.

Max was unprepared for what he saw. It all happened too fast. Or was it in slow motion? Maybe he just imagined it was Lucy—gentle Lucy with her smooth, silky coat. One fragile ear lay motionless against her graceful neck.

The man stepped back. "My boy was walking his dog," he said, "and they found her dead below the footpath. Hit and run, I guess. Maybe internal injuries."

Max cut him off. "Thank you," he said. He didn't seem to want any words. He felt Lucy's soft muzzle, stroked her withers and the full length of her tail. His hand came to rest on her side, as if hoping her eyes might open at his friendly touch.

He lifted the small dog. She seemed lighter than ever. There was no need for help, but the man stayed to be useful. Together they dug a grave near the birdbath in the upper boxwood garden.

It was one of the areas Lucy had kept free of squirrels. She had often amused Max by stumping along, barking valiantly at the place a squirrel had once been.

When the turf was placed carefully over the grave, they shook hands. Max walked his neighbor to the car and thanked him again.

The man had mentioned a footpath. It ran alongside the narrow road. There were few reasons for traveling that route, but cars sometimes got away with speeding. Maybe it was someone on the way to the cottage. Mimi could have gone that way. Clearly the accident happened recently. If it was an accident. Aside from Hetty or Katrinka, he hadn't noticed anyone coming or going. Max looked toward the gate.

He was thinking this way when Katrinka suddenly came from nowhere. She winked at him. "You're in a real trance," she said.

She tilted her head. "I brought you a photograph. It was in a box Daddy told me to throw out." She put her hands on her hips. "I won't part with any of Daddy's things without a fight!" She laughed sweetly as if to remind Max she was far too dainty to wear boxing gloves.

He frowned. "You could at least get new furniture. Phil's been gone three years. Joseph could use something that suits his height."

Katrinka handed him the picture.

He glanced at it. "I have two copies already," he said. "If this is all you've found in the box, it's safe to throw it all out."

"I've just begun to sort through it," she said, "but maybe you're right, Max." Her little pearly-white teeth implied he always was.

CHAPTER FOUR

"The things Daddy wrote about elephants—they're everywhere in the files. Joseph had no idea how brilliant he was."

Max handed back the picture, and she tucked it in her pocket.

"I really didn't think it would make you gloomy," she said.

"No, no." His hand brushed away her statement. "I'm sure you've seen a little lame dog around here."

"A dog? Max honey, you know I spend full time minding my own business." Her eyes blinked and opened wide with innocence. "But what about it?"

"Looks like she was killed by a car," he said. He looked in the direction Lucy had been found. "How could anyone do that and just drive away?"

Katrinka tossed her hair. "Maybe they did it on purpose," she said, turning toward the gatehouse.

As Katrinka flounced away, Max saw Mimi drive up. He watched her Lamborghini circle to the back entrance. Didn't she see him? She could be purposely avoiding him. Perhaps she knew something about Lucy's death. Mimi would have reason to be glad the dog was dead. She wanted to get rid of Ignatz, and with Lucy gone, there was nothing to make him stick around.

Max clenched his teeth and dragged his feet to the door.

Evidence

Katrinka went home to the gatehouse. She sat at the kitchen table and continued sorting through the box. For the most part, she could see why Phil had wanted her to discard it. All the photographs she found were inferior duplicates of those already in a scrapbook.

The picture of her mother made her sad, but she wasn't sure why. Maybe Katrinka was afraid of growing up to look the same. Her neck was short, and her head seemed to come directly out of her shoulders. When Katrinka was a child, her mother's misshapen body had embarrassed her.

Daddy, she thought, *did you send me away because I was mean to Mother?* She stared at the picture, wishing for another chance.

"Mother," she whispered, "would I still pretend not to know you?" As tears gathered, Katrinka blinked them away and tried not to think about it. She hid the picture at the bottom of the pile.

Her fingers closed around a manila envelope. Quickly she pulled it out and inspected it on both sides. She had a feeling this could be an important discovery. It was taped closed, and a large "X" was scribbled on the front.

Inside the envelope, she found a letter addressed to Phil. Something was attached to it with a paper clip. It was a note from Max to her father—an apology which she read and read again.

Katrinka now had shocking evidence. It was more useful than she could have hoped.

When she heard Joseph at the front door, Katrinka was quick to hide the contents of the envelope, but slow to acknowledge him. She barely looked up after he entered. By inventing a casual sort of cough, she hoped to disguise her triumphant joy.

"You look happy," he said.

"Hmm? Oh, yes, I *am*." She thought fast and came up with a convincing reason for her gleeful expression. "I don't think Ignatz will be around much longer," she said. "His dog got hit by a car. I don't see why everybody's all worked up about it. It's just a dog."

She rolled her eyes. "All I hear is Lucy this and Lucy that, all the time. I'm glad it's dead." To prove it, she played her dimples for him.

Joseph turned his face away.

CHAPTER FOUR

She continued to speak with conviction. "Dogs can be a mess," she said, "and so smelly."

Her silence was the most Joseph could hope for, but Katrinka disappointed him with another outburst. "Good riddance to both of them," she said.

Joseph had come home planning a heavy discussion with his wife, but perhaps this was not the time. Was there reason to suspect her of hitting Lucy? If he faced her, she might sense his suspicion, so he kept his frown to himself and walked away.

When Katrinka was sure Joseph was beyond where he could hear, she called Morgan. He might be working late at the law office.

He was. Morgan answered the phone himself. "Honeybun," she said, "I just wanted to make sure our sweet Hetty is okay. I heard about the dog she hit."

"Dog? What are you saying?"

"You mean . . . you mean she didn't tell you?" Katrinka sighed with heartfelt sympathy. "I was *sure* she would turn to you first—*her own husband!* But don't you worry. I imagine she'll confess before long. The poor dear—she must have been thinking about something else while she was driving. It *is* hard to be careful on that road. Bless her heart, she's probably not the best driver, the way she gets lost all the time."

"Thank you, Katrinka. I appreciate your concern. I'm sure I'll hear all about it when I get home."

"Oh, dear," she said. "The more I think about it, maybe you won't! It's obvious Hetty doesn't want you to find out. But it's only natural, if she feels ashamed. Promise me you'll forgive her, Morgan honey. And please forget I told you. I could cut my tongue out! Maybe she hasn't learned what I've always known—that it's best to be honest."

Katrinka heard Joseph coming back toward the kitchen and quietly hung up the phone without saying goodbye. Maybe Morgan would think they got disconnected.

She hoped so. But it didn't matter now, as long as Joseph didn't know about the phone call. The important thing was winning Joseph's confidence. Yet somehow, Hetty was always in the way. It was annoying the way Joseph saw Hetty as a good influence. And that he wanted them to be friends. That would never happen.

Hetty had too many irritating qualities. For one thing, whenever Katrinka was sad, Hetty sensed it. Was it some sort of witchcraft? And there was something else. Katrinka couldn't understand why Hetty said nice things about her. How could anything she said possibly be sincere?

Often, when Katrinka had no place else to turn, she longed for their friendship to be real. She could speak openly to Hetty about her worries and loneliness. And whenever Hetty listened, offering counsel and comfort, it was tempting to think of her as a friend. Fortunately, she was able to convince herself it was just a ploy. Hetty must be pretending to care so she would somehow seem *superior*.

Katrinka knew Joseph wasn't looking at her. She waited in vain for some kind words of attention, hoping his heart would soften if he were to glance her way even briefly. She posed gracefully against the pink flowered wallpaper of the kitchen. Surely he could see that Hetty Morganthal could not compete. Even if that didn't work, she would find some way to get the upper hand.

Her eyes avoided looking at the manila envelope, in case Joseph might notice. He would never approve of her keeping it. But Katrinka knew the value of the written confession from Max. It would give her control over her destiny.

Worse Than Nothing

Marian confronted the refrigerator. Leaf had offered to clean it out, and she was embarrassed to know he thought it was that urgent. Maybe she could manage it herself.

CHAPTER FOUR

If only she could think of something less overwhelming to do. Wasn't there any housekeeping project that might reward her with a sense of accomplishment? She doubted it.

While considering her options, she read the newspaper. Even the Warren Commission had an easier task; someday their investigation would be over and done, whereas the refrigerator was a never-ending source of concern.

Finally Marian decided on another project. With a sigh of resolve, she went to the living room and plugged in the Electrolux vacuum.

Leaf had been the one to vacuum ever since their marriage. He once showed Marian an enlarged picture of a dust mite. The sight of such a monster would terrify a normal person into vacuuming. Then Leaf worried that maybe it seemed like he was hinting for her to do it. He certainly hadn't meant it that way, but he apologized just in case.

Before long, Marian was on the phone with Hetty. "My vacuum doesn't suck anything up anymore. I had to pick up crumbs by hand and feed them into it. Maybe it's because I've never emptied it before."

"Oh," said Hetty, "do you want me to walk you through it?"

"Please, if you don't mind," said Marian.

She moved the trashcan and the vacuum closer to where the phone was attached to the kitchen wall. Now she could hear Hetty's instructions. Long intervals of clunking sounds were required to free some nonworking part of the vacuum. It became entangled with the telephone cord and tipped over.

Marian checked with Hetty between muffled grunts. "An anthropologist would have a heyday. You wouldn't believe the stuff I found in the bag," she said. "Ah ha! So that's what happened to the cat!"

Hetty laughed. "I think putting it back together will be the easy part."

Marian already had a glowing sense of accomplishment. When Hetty asked if it was reassembled yet, she said, "Wait till I show Leaf what I've done! Can you hang on while I see how it works?" She sounded positively gleeful.

Hetty was happy to wait. She heard vacuum noises followed by heavy breathing.

"Uh oh, it still doesn't do anything," said Marian. "No, wait. I was wrong. Now it spreads dirt and stuff back on the carpet."

"Well," said Hetty, "that's progress, but it's definitely the wrong kind. It means your hose is clogged. Here's what you'll need to do: straighten out a wire hanger and leave a hook at the end . . ."

Discouraged, Marian sat down, but with a new self-awareness. She had identified her enemy, and its name was Electrolux.

"Thanks for your help," she sighed, "but I give up. Maybe Leaf will fix it." She flopped over the counter and changed the subject. "Tell me, is Freydis sleeping better?

"Not much," said Hetty. "She gets night and day confused. Every idea we have is worse than doing nothing at all."

Hetty was tired from the nights of interrupted sleep. But she intended to make some pink cupcakes for Katrinka, and she said so. "I'd better get started," she said. "When I last saw Katrinka, she seemed more open to a visit."

Marian had nothing to say at first, but when Hetty questioned her silence, it came out. "I don't know, Hetty. Maybe it's a little complicated right now."

"But if she could use a friend," said Hetty, "I mustn't worry about complications."

Marian seemed hesitant to explain it, but she said, "Well, from something Joseph says, it might be best to do nothing."

"Maybe I should take that chance," said Hetty, "even if I risk wasting my time. I can live with myself better if I've tried."

"Yes. Yes, I know you feel that way. I love that about you. But if it would be *worse* than doing nothing—if they see you as part of the problem . . ."

"Oh!" said Hetty, "I don't mean to be a problem . . . to cause any trouble. I didn't realize . . . thank you. Thank you for telling me . . ." Her voice trailed off, and she hung up the phone. She put away the sugar and the cake flour. Her finger slowly went around and around in a well of the muffin tin. Hetty thought of Marian's vacuum—spreading dirt, instead of picking it up.

Is that how I affect people? What's the point of anything? What good am I if I make things worse instead of better?

The Strange Object

It was late when Morgan got home. Darkness was creeping in close behind him, and the cottage was strangely quiet.

Freydis sat in the window looking out anxiously at the gathering gloom. "When is that nice young man coming for me?" she asked. "We're going to have a party by the oak forest. His little dog likes to bark at the squirrels."

Morgan kissed her on the forehead. "Would you like me to turn on some music for you?" he asked.

"No, thank you, dear. He'll be coming soon. I'll just wait here. We're . . . we're going somewhere." She seemed uncertain.

Morgan patted her hand. "To have a party?" he asked.

"Yes . . . yes, that's it." She looked up at him in confusion. "You're Morgan," she said. She appeared relieved to have that straight.

In the kitchen, Hetty had left a plate of food for him, but Morgan turned on the lamp in the hall and mounted the stairs instead. To the right of the landing, Pippa's door was ajar. Morgan removed his shoes so his footsteps wouldn't disturb her sleep.

It seemed she had been waiting for him to come home, and her pale lashes opened just a little. "Daddy," she whispered.

In the half-light, he could just make out a strange object in her hand. It was Lucy's collar.

"Where did you get that, honey?"

"It's mine. I found it."

"Where was it?"

"Under Mommy's chair," she said.

He lingered there, watching until her eyes drooped and her breathing was steady. Pippa didn't notice when he took the dog collar from her and replaced it with a floppy stuffed lamb. Nor did she see him hide it behind the false front high on top of the cabinet.

He returned to straighten the tangled sheets. Slowly he left her side and climbed the stairs to the loft.

That's where he found Hetty. She lay curled up on the bed with her back to him. After waiting unsuccessfully for her to acknowledge his presence, Morgan left quietly, avoiding the squeaky floorboards.

CHAPTER FIVE

Emptiness

Morgan went downstairs, and all was still. Hetty closed her eyes against the sick emptiness of the room. She remained curled up on the bed and thought about her disappointment.

I heard you walk upstairs, Morgan. I knew you were coming to look for me, and I counted your steps. When I got to six, you stopped at Pippa's room. I waited and counted again.

Couldn't you hear my heart beating? It was all about you. I had to hold my breath to control my anticipation—to parcel out my excitement carefully, so I wouldn't burst with need for you.

My thoughts prepared me to see you in a different way—new and fresh. I thought of the time last year, when I was buying groceries at Safeway, and you came in for a newspaper. It was just by chance we were there at the same time.

Suddenly you came near, and the joy welled up inside me. I thought everyone in the world must sense my feelings. Even the cornstarch, cabbages, and tuna fish must feel it.

Your eyes crinkled in the corners with the same smile I've known since I was a child. But because I never saw you in that very place, it seemed like I'd never seen you at all. Or like we had met in some lifetime long ago, in a bright and holy place.

One time I saw my teacher in the drugstore. It startled me that she would need dental floss like regular people do. I had to hide behind Mother while I figured it out.

But it was different seeing you. I wanted to run through the aisles with you that very moment and say, "Stop what you're doing, everyone. Here he is! This is the man I had in mind when I reached for the canned peaches on the top shelf. He was the one in my thoughts as I passed the watermelons and remembered how we laughed, spitting out seeds together."

My hands wanted to feel your face to see if it was really you. It was only three in the afternoon, and I wanted to tell all the shoppers, "See how his beard is already growing in? I get to feel it whenever I like."

I wanted to announce over the intercom, "We have something special today in the bakery section: the person most dear to me—the father of my child."

I know you saw me here on the bed. Could you tell I was awake? By staying still, was it the same as lying to you? I didn't mean it that way.

You were disappointed in me when I didn't tell your parents about Ignatz. Maybe this was another disappointment—the way I pretended not to hear you. If that's why you left, I know you won't speak of it. You'll be kind and spare my feelings.

I remember your kindness when my school put you on the dance committee. Did you dance with me out of pity? No one else would. I made all the boys look short, but you didn't seem to mind.

Of course Joseph Ostler was taller, but when I was with Joseph, I always pretended he was you.

Katrinka says your feelings for me are mostly pity. She's right about a lot of things. For one, I know less than nothing about being before the public.

Oh, Morgan! You've always known when I need you. Why

didn't you sit on the bed the way I expected and turn me toward you? I was desperate for your comfort.

I needed to feel your arms around me and hear you say, "I'm home, Hetty." I was eager to say I love you in a thousand ways.

Now the room is empty—like a party that didn't happen. If you make paper hats for all the guests you invite, and nobody comes, you can bury them deep in the trash. That way you don't have to look at them anymore and be reminded of how you felt.

But your absence is too big to bury. It's everywhere. I feel it on my skin where you didn't touch me. I smell it in the memory of your scent, and I see it in the darkness that would have disappeared at the sight of you.

A Short Walk

In the morning, Joseph suggested to Katrinka that they should go for a walk. He had a few things to say, and the fresh air would keep his thinking clear. They could be back in time to leave for the office.

Unfortunately, a breeze was blowing. Rather than have it mess up her hair, Katrinka wanted to turn back after only a few steps. She was experimenting with some little spit curls at the temples. Joseph asked what they had to do with spit. She declared that was the silliest question she had ever heard, which led him to believe she didn't know either.

When they reentered the gatehouse, Joseph indicated a place in the living room where they could sit in two facing chairs. He began directly. "First of all," he said, "I was disturbed by your reaction when Lucy was run over."

"Oh, Joseph! I don't know what was I thinking. I don't really feel that way. Honest I don't!"

He hesitated to continue. Her eyes were large and luminous with sincerity. At least they were luminous with something. "I almost believe your lies," he said, "and when I do, it makes me feel dirty."

"Honey," said Katrinka, "if this little talk is because I'm gaining weight . . . or getting wrinkles . . ."

"What's the matter with you, Trink? I'm talking about what's real. Cut out the wrinkle nonsense." He shook his head.

Surprise could have been responsible for her confused expression. She now wished to clarify her earlier unkind words. "It's just that I have reason to believe Hetty killed the dog," she said, "and I thought by making you suspect *me* because of what I said, it would protect *Hetty* from suspicion."

"I don't believe you, Katrinka. You've been mean-spirited with her, and she's never done anything to hurt you. Maybe I just loved you for what I hoped you would become—for the way your father thought you were, somewhere inside. I was satisfied with waiting for you to grow up. All I've ever had of you was your honesty. Now that's gone. Your pretty face is nothing but a mask."

"No, no, Joseph, sweetheart! You don't understand. I'm yours completely! I absolutely worship the ground you walk on. And about me being pretty—I do it all for you."

He composed himself by tapping his heel up and down. "You only want what you can't have. That's the one reason you came crawling to Australia to marry me. I won't take part in that game anymore. No matter how much you wish I were Morgan Morganthal, I never will be. And you can't make me jealous by talking that way."

The horror of her situation showed in Katrinka's face. She had never been rejected like this before. She clapped her hands over her ears with no apparent concern for the little spit curls. "No! Don't talk like that!" she wailed. "Please, I'll do anything you say!"

Joseph was unmoved. "I don't want to control you," he said. "I want you to control yourself."

CHAPTER FIVE

Katrinka sobbed as if her heart would break. Her hands were ready to reach for him, but Joseph showed no interest in her needs.

He tapped his fingers on the arm of the chair. "I'm sorry." His next words were meant to be more helpful. "You know the best thing you could do? Make friends with Hetty. She'll want to be helpful. She cares about you."

Katrinka's spine straightened immediately, and in no time she took control of her corner of the stage. The part she played stunned her audience.

"Darling," she hissed, "I just thought of something. When Hetty was in high school, you didn't go back home to Australia like you were going to. You changed plans and stayed in Marian's house instead. It was to court Hetty, wasn't it?" She laughed. "It strikes me as amusing."

She rolled her eyes. "You can talk all you want about how she helps people get along so well. It seems to me that little meddler messes up everybody's plans. That's her reputation."

A distinct sadness was in Joseph's eyes, and he sounded defeated. "Don't monkey with Hetty's reputation," he said.

Katrinka tilted her head and smiled adorably at her husband. "Why should you care?" she said. "She never cared about you. I find it ironic, when she wasn't as popular as me. And as for her reputation—she'd better look out for herself, the same as the rest of us," she sniffed. "I'm going to the office."

Joseph would go see his sister Marian.

The Chance Meeting

Katrinka said she was going to the office, but she had something else in mind. She knew Max liked to supervise the workmen when they cleaned the swimming pool. He would be strolling over there about now. With a seemingly casual grace, Katrinka made a point of meeting him there.

"I was just thinking," she said wistfully, "as I so often do, about your wonderful partnership with Daddy."

Max nodded and shaded his eyes with his hands.

After a little sigh, she said, "I'm so amazed to learn how famous Daddy *could* have been." Her words were quickly followed by a crooked little smile of apology. "Oh, dear! I shouldn't have said anything! You're such a darling, and I wouldn't want you to blame yourself for what you did! But isn't it wonderful to know *other* people appreciated him?"

Max frowned. He turned a deep red and seemed unable to speak for an awkward length of time. He looked toward the pool as if it might have been relocated in the interval. At last he said, "About what I did to Phil—Hetty couldn't have told you."

The statement seemed to hurt Katrinka; how could Max doubt Hetty would confide in her! "Max honey, why on earth would you say that?" She blinked her eyes with sweet innocence. "Hetty and I are so close!" She squeezed two fingers together to suggest they shared intimate secrets. "She's like a sister to me."

Max thought of something to say. "You could argue Hetty's your neice. After all, her father married Joseph's sister."

Katrinka pouted. "Marian's only Joseph's *step*sister. I *refuse* to be Hetty's aunt," she said.

Soon her expression mellowed somewhat, and her little pink lips smiled with a degree of forgiveness. After all, Max probably didn't mean to make her feel old. He was just making conversation.

"Daddy was so fond of you," she said, "and you know *I* am. It's been hard getting rid of Daddy's things, but you were right, I should have changed the furniture to fit Joseph long ago." She sighed as if to imply that her marriage would be blissfully free of difficulties had Max suggested it sooner.

"And about the stuff I was supposed to toss out," she said, "maybe I should have."

The long friendship of Max and her father had been strong. Maybe someday the evidence in the manila envelope should be destroyed.

Someday, but not just yet.

Cheddar Cheese

Marian sat before the open refrigerator door and surveyed the crowded contents. When Leaf had opened it earlier, a half-eaten apple tumbled out. Fitting the apple back in the right place was a challenge, but he slammed the door in time to hold back the avalanche of hardboiled eggs and green beans.

Just as a wedge of moldy cheese fell at Marian's feet, the doorbell rang. She left her chore with no reluctance. It was Joseph grinning at her from the doorstep. "Morning, Sis! What are you up to?"

"Hey there!" she said with enthusiasm. She avoided mention of the refrigerator. "Come on in."

As they went toward the kitchen, the gaping refrigerator screamed out to be closed. Marian didn't notice it, but Joseph did. He closed it while she picked up the errant chunk of cheese and tossed it in the trash.

"I wouldn't throw that out," said Joseph. "It just *looks* bad. Cut off the mold, and it'll be good inside."

Marian retrieved it and gave him a knife so he could perform the operation himself. Meanwhile, she moved a pan from one chair and books from another so they could sit at the table.

"What brings you here?" she asked. "Not that you ever need a reason." She smiled.

"I'm hoping," he said, "that you'll look out for Katrinka."

She nodded, but voiced a friendly concern. "That sister-in-law of mine is like a herd of kangaroos. But I'll do my best."

He became serious. "I'm leaving for the elephant sanctuary."

"Oh? You mean it's not quite as hot in Africa as it is here?"

Joseph laughed. "You said it!"

"How long will you be gone?" asked Marian.

He paused and looked out the window. "Indefinitely."

Marian's quizzical expression spread to her mouth, but she was speechless.

"I'll be leaving quietly in a couple of days," he said. "Katrinka doesn't know about it yet."

Marian shook her head. "I'm surprised at Max and Morgan. Why would they ask you to do such a thing?"

"They didn't."

Now Marian understood. "Oh, it was your idea. So it's that bad. Is there anything I can do?"

His silence meant *no* but he stared at the cheese as if considering his earlier words—and whether Katrinka was still good inside too.

"You know Hetty would want to help any way she can," said Marian. "She has a way of smoothing things out."

Joseph shook his head. "I mentioned that again, just this morning," he said. "From Katrinka's reaction, I still think Hetty's part of the problem."

Marian folded her arms and said what she thought. "You've done all you can, Joseph. You and your wife just don't have anything in common."

"Yes, we do," he said. "Katrinka and I . . . we both love Katrinka.

Ignatz Returns

Max answered a rather tentative knock at the door. Beverley Ignatz Gorman stood drooping in front of him.

"Uh, Mrs. Fairburn, she thinks people oughta say 'thank you' when folks is nice to them. That's what extinguishes a

CHAPTER FIVE

gentlemen from those what ain't . . . I mean, you know. I got to figuring I oughta do like that." He forced a nervous cough.

"I would of came back sooner," he said, "but I run outa bus money. You done what you could for my Lucy. I get that you won't want me back. Leastwise not now. Now that she's, you know . . . " Ignatz pulled his cap down to hide his eyes.

"So," said Max, "you know what happened to Lucy?"

"Well," Ignatz shifted his weight from one foot to the other. "Here's how it was. Me and Lucy drove Mrs. Fairburn over to the footpath to have us a party. I bought this cake to pretend like it was her birthday. There was this real terrific spot where we could see the water. Then I come back to get them from out the car.

"I brung me a leash so's Lucy could be out in the world and bark at the squirrels. Crazy dog! She was a real pertector."

Ignatz faced the ground for a time. "You never gonna see a squirrel come around to chew on us. Man, I mean *never!*" He lowered his cap again. Max waited quietly.

"To start with," said Ignatz, "they was both sitting in the front seat with me. Lucy ain't much of a athlete, but I guess she was more stronger than we thought. That crazy girl . . . she jumps in the back seat real quick and gets herself a chicken leg." He shook his head slowly from side to side.

"Then she chokes on it. Mrs. Fairburn, she's is crying like it's her fault, she's so mixed up. But it weren't no use, it was over. Lucy, she dies while I got her like this in my arms. I took off her collar so I'd never forget . . . stupid collar," he mumbled.

"We put her a little ways off the road. By a big rock. Just like a monument. I didn't want no dirt touching my Lucy. We had us a real two-people service with religion and all. I even said this thing I heard about heaven. Then Mrs. Fairburn, she put flower petals over Lucy while I conjugated about what's next.

"I got to wishing it wasn't real about Lucy being dead, and that give me a idea. I instigated real hard about how Mrs.

Fairburn oughta forget what happened . . . like she does with lots of stuff. I even prayed it in my head . . . you know, with all the religion we just got done using.

"I took her back to the cottage, and she cries when I tell her I gotta go away. I says Lucy was the only reason you let me stay here at your place.

"Anyways, I got done praying how she could maybe wash it out of her brain, and you know what? She wonders could she keep Lucy's collar. I pretty near said I want it myself, but Mrs. Fairburn up and says can she keep it to remember me by. *Me*. She wants to remember *me*, for crying out loud."

Mimi emerged from the shadows where she had been listening. She joined her husband and said, "Come in, Ignatz."

His head jerked up.

"We'll set up the projector for you," she said.

His Protective Care

Morgan tried to concentrate on mowing the lawn, but his mind wandered to the image of Hetty lying curled up on the bed. Had she needed him? Maybe she wanted the feeling of security he could provide, and he failed her. He should have whispered in her ear to find out. Instead, he had walked away to let her rest. But regrets could serve no useful purpose.

He wasn't sure why he had hidden the dog collar. He supposed he did it instinctively to protect Hetty, in case anyone should suspect her of Lucy's death.

Morgan stopped to wipe the sweat from his face and neck. The exertion of pushing and steering the mower by its wooden handle was, to him, an essential part of caring for the land. The satisfaction would not have been the same with a gas mower.

The smell of earth and fresh cut grass seemed to strengthen the ties he and Hetty shared with the outdoors. He thought

CHAPTER FIVE

of his time in the Forest Service. He missed the intensity of fighting fires. Even the exhaustion.

When Morgan turned at the end of each row, he listened to the birds calling and looked into the cool depths of the forest. From the time Hetty was twelve years old, she was drawn to Olive Witch Forest. She thrived in the company of Hannah, the massive tree. Hannah was her refuge and confidante.

Morgan smiled to recall his first encounter with Hetty. His little sister Melinda had brought her home as a guest. From the moment of their meeting, Hetty's shy sweetness seemed to reach far into his future—as if asking to be encircled in his care. Soon, his primal desire to protect her became a powerful force.

In time, his increasing drive to provide for Hetty and keep her safe gave dimension to Morgan's life. It defined his manhood.

By the time Morgan finished a fourth row with the lawnmower, the heat of the day convinced him he needed to go inside and change into more comfortable clothes.

He entered through the kitchen. Hetty stood at the stove, where sizzling and stirring sounds indicated dinner was well under way. Pippa and Freydis sat together at the table, sorting through photographs. When Morgan winked at Pippa, she laughed and tried unsuccessfully to do the same. Instead, they ended with pat-a-cake, a game she had mastered.

He watched Hetty at work in her white apron. The sight of his wife as a cook and homemaker warmed Morgan with continual pleasure. Until their marriage, such things were unfamiliar to him. His mother had delegated all kitchen duties entirely to the servants.

The telephone rang, and Morgan answered it. It was Marian. As they spoke, he turned to watch Hetty.

Marian said, "I'm worried about what I said to Hetty. I have complete confidence in her diplomacy. It's not that. I'm not sure why Joseph wants her to stay clear of Katrinka."

Even though Marian now wanted to soften the effect of whatever she had said earlier, Morgan was sure she must have meant well at the time. Still, he appreciated her thoughtfulness.

Hetty removed some fragrant rolls from the oven and tasted whatever she was stirring. She added a pinch of something or other. Not salt or pepper. He would have recognized those. The whole process was deliciously incomprehensible.

Morgan turned his attention to thanking Marian before saying goodbye, then sat at the table. He shuffled through the old photographs without really seeing them. He didn't notice the floppy hats decorated with birds and flowers. Or the babies that were blurry because they didn't hold still for the camera. He didn't even see the cars with their proud owners posing on the fenders. All Morgan could see was Hetty. He wanted her to be happy. Always before, when she needed him, he was able to fill that need. At least he thought so.

Slowly, he rose and walked up behind her as she stood at the stove. She was stirring something that smelled buttery. He put both arms around her waist, as if to say, *please need me. Will you tell me if you do?* But he kept his thoughts to himself.

What did Marian say to upset her? Why doesn't Hetty tell me about it?

What was it? Oh, I remember—she wants Hetty to stay away from Katrinka. But that doesn't make sense.

Hetty turned to face him, and he held her close. There were so many things to say, if only they were alone. He might ask about her sadness, or why her thoughts had seemed so far away. That worried him, and it had for some time. Hetty seemed tense.

"It's good you want to help Katrinka," he said. Then something else occurred to him in the silence that followed.

Joseph's a good man—very likeable. Maybe Hetty wishes I could be like him. Years ago, he was interested in Hetty. Seriously interested. Katrinka must know that. Maybe she's resentful and jealous. If so, I see how having Hetty around could complicate things.

CHAPTER FIVE

Morgan's dark eyes clouded over and looked even more serious than usual. He felt somber and lackluster compared to the tall, easy-going Joseph. Hetty's eyes were moist, and Morgan wondered if her sadness was because Joseph had left that morning.

She deserves to be around cheerful people like Joseph. Should I bring him home? Does Hetty think I wanted to send him away? Joseph doesn't want me to tell people it was his idea to leave.

Suddenly, an explosion of flames shook the room. A jagged ball of fire raged from the frying pan as the butter and oil ignited. Its searing hot fingers leapt to Hetty's hair, and she looked to Morgan in terror. Forked tongues of the inferno blazed across the stove and up the wall.

Snatching Hetty from the scorching heat, Morgan smothered her burning hair with his hands. He worked with swift confidence. Instinct increased the speed of his skillful movements. Glancing around the room, he grabbed the baking sheet with the rolls and tossed it over the pan. He turned off the fan and made sure Hetty's hair and clothes were not smoldering.

Wide-eyed, Pippa froze in place, clinging to Freydis.

Morgan surveyed the damage. Hetty's hair had a gaping space in back. The rolls were scattered across the floor. Only two remained on the baking sheet that now covered the frying pan. Smoke and the smell of burnt hair choked the air.

Hetty couldn't hide her admiration. "What if you hadn't been here!" she said. "It all happened so fast . . . you did everything at once."

At the sink, Morgan ran cool water over his hands. "I'm so sorry," he said. "It was a beautiful dinner."

The thick smoke drove them all outdoors. Pippa guided Freydis to the bench in the shade of the rose trellis.

Hetty worried about Morgan's burns and brought out a pan of water to cool his left hand. Her genuine appreciation and amazement reduced his pain.

She lay against him in the hammock—her head nestled against his chest. Morgan savored her softness and the feelings it evoked. What miracle had placed her in his care?

They listened to Pippa's musical chatter mingled with bird songs. The squeak of their hammock was a metronome for the woodland creatures to follow or disregard as they wished.

The chatter came closer as Pippa scampered toward the hammock. Soon her little elbows poked everywhere to find a comfortable position between her parents. Tipping some water from the pan, she wriggled close to Morgan's ear. "I don't like fire," she said. For emphasis, she pressed her father's face between her chubby hands. The multiple ways she announced her opinion convinced them of her sincerity.

When she seemed satisfied with the delivery of her message, Pippa hopped back to Freydis, mostly on one foot.

"I'll get more water," said Hetty. But she hoped Morgan would listen for her unspoken words: *Don't let me go, Morgan. I could lie next to you like this forever. I don't need Hannah. It's you I need.*

Morgan's answer was clear and quiet, affirming the understanding of one soul for another. He flashed a smile and said simply, "Stay."

Make Her Squirm

It took time to set things right in the smoky kitchen, but Hetty hummed while she worked. Nothing could diminish her contentment. She smiled at the black and crusted frying pan.

Hetty's thoughts wandered to the gatehouse, because she knew Katrinka was not as fortunate. She picked up the phone and dialed her number, before losing courage. In Joseph's absence, perhaps Katrinka needed to feel appreciated.

"I hope everything's all right," she said.

CHAPTER FIVE

Katrinka sounded subdued. "It's so hard for Joseph, being away from me, and he hasn't even arrived there yet. He's trying so hard to be strong," she said.

"I'm so sorry," said Hetty. "Then maybe you won't mind thinking about something else. I'll be interviewing Tilly Teller, in two weeks. You know her better than I do. I'm sure you'll have some good ideas—that is, if you're willing to help me out."

"Oh, yes!" Katrinka sounded quite eager to help plan for the interview. "What do you have in mind so far?"

Hetty was pleased. Maybe her instinct to include Katrinka was correct. "Well," she said, "Tilly has a reputation for giving wonderful parties. I could ask her to share a few secrets of success."

Katrinka sighed. "No, no. You'll have your listeners falling asleep. They'll be absolutely *snoring*! You should ask about the party she *didn't* have—the one she canceled to attend her favorite uncle's funeral." She laughed. "Tilly didn't even *have* an uncle! She really canceled because Morgan couldn't be there. The governor needed him to ride in a motorcade with him. Tilly was *furious* when her star guest couldn't come."

Katrinka made a sweet little humming sound. "And of course it made no sense for me to go to it without Morgan. We looked so terrific together."

Hetty paused and mentioned a more comfortable idea. "I thought I'd ask Tilly how she happened to start writing her column for the paper."

"Isn't that a little too obvious?" said Katrinka. "It's just what she'll expect."

Hetty could see her point. "You can see why I need your help," she said.

Katrinka made more happy sounds. "Yes, you do, because I know what works. And believe me, Hetty dear, all your questions—they've *got* to throw her off guard!"

"Oh . . . I couldn't do that," said Hetty.

"You've got to, if you want to keep your audience," said Katrinka. "For example, ask about the scandal that got her started in the first place. Her father would have been in trouble with the law, but Tilly found some dirt on the man who was going to expose him. The article she wrote was a very clever threat."

"But that sounds like blackmail," said Hetty.

"You don't need to use a dirty word like that, honey. Just ask her. I promise it'll make her squirm."

"Oh . . . that's not my goal."

"Well, it should be," said Katrinka. "She writes a gossip column. You'd only be giving her what she deserves. People get away with whatever they can, and Tilly's no exception, bless her heart."

Hetty thought of the unkind things Tilly had said about her over the last few years. *Could Katrinka be right?*

Too Trusting

Hetty's hand was still on the phone when it rang again. Max had disturbing news about Ignatz. In silent disappointment, Hetty listened and took notes on a pad of yellow legal paper.

At last she responded. "So . . . you say he was going through your drawers and closets. Mostly upstairs. You're sure you got clear photos?" She doodled at the bottom of the page. "I'd like to think about this, if you'll hold off contacting the police. Thank you for telling me first, Max."

She told Morgan the news when he came in. He was sorry but not surprised. "It's good Ignatz didn't hear the camera and do something violent," he said.

"That wouldn't be like him," said Hetty.

Morgan shook his head. "We don't know that."

Hetty felt defensive, but above all, as if something beautiful was slipping away. The friendship between Ignatz and Freydis was more important to her than she had realized. But Hetty questioned her own intuition. Could such an unlikely relationship have been real?

Pressing hard with her pencil as she spoke, she doodled in heavy concentric circles. "You told Ignatz people should be considered innocent. And unless there's proof otherwise, we need to assume they are. That was a new idea to him. Besides," she said, "shouldn't we think that way even outside of the law? And isn't it a good policy to trust whenever possible?"

Morgan plowed ahead. "We've given him plenty of trust. Maybe he didn't deserve it. What excuse will he invent for going through Dad's personal belongings? I say he's up to no good."

Hetty didn't give up. "But Max hasn't found anything missing," she said.

"Of course not. If something's missing, you can't find it, because it's not there any more. That's the problem."

She forced a smile to acknowledge his humor. "But not finding it doesn't mean he took it," she said.

Morgan seemed frustrated. "When you don't find anything is missing, it only means you don't know what missing thing to look for," he said. "If we found it, that doesn't make him innocent, either—even if I ought to assume he is. If nothing else, he's guilty of trespassing. His past record doesn't inspire a whole lot of confidence."

That was obvious enough to silence Hetty until she said, "Can't we forgive his trespassing? Aunt Freydis is so happy to have him back."

"You're too trusting, Hetty. He only came back because he was out of money."

Hetty thought of Ignatz and his efforts to change. Might this incident destroy his progress toward a new life? She closed her eyes to straighten her thinking. Was she being naïve?

Something Katrinka said came to her mind. *Be realistic,* she said. *Just because you're such a goody-goody doesn't mean everyone else is too.*

Hetty wished fervently to see the good in Ignatz; however, wanting it didn't make it true. Of course Max and Morgan were right. Maybe she should get in step with the real world. Ignatz had returned to steal money from the Morganthals, and there was no excuse for it.

Where optimism had ruled, Hetty now felt a dull ache. She had nurtured hope at her own peril. Why hadn't she seen it would turn sour? She faced Morgan squarely. "I suppose . . . I suppose you're saying . . . " But Hetty couldn't finish.

Her eyes were blank and lifeless. Her mouth refused to put Morgan's intentions into words. If a decision suggested itself, he would have to voice it.

Morgan turned and leaned stiffly against the table, clenching his fist. Optimism vanished. Hetty stared out the window at the darkening forest. She wanted to run to Hannah's comforting branches.

CHAPTER SIX

The Crystal Ball

Katrinka looked out the gatehouse window, as if searching for hope in the gathering gloom. But loneliness snuffed out the least glimmer of optimism. Had Joseph really said those awful things? She tried hard to imagine them away so her eyes would not look puffy from crying.

Every day, she put her full energy into her work at LuvCon. But it was the long, lonely evenings that exhausted her. She removed her eyelashes and her pink shoes. To lift her spirits, Katrinka kept a box of chocolate creams available. But even that didn't help much. She lay down on the bed.

Rolling toward Joseph's side of the bed, she laid her hand where his head ought to be and pretended he was still there. A big tear wet her pillow, and she squeezed her eyes closed. His cheerful grin was vivid in her memory, and she could still hear the words of his proposal—the proposal she had at first dismissed.

You're a high maintenance woman, Trink. You're so much trouble, I'd like to get started right away.

She whispered, "Joseph, you still love me, don't you?"

But only one vision came to her mind. She could picture him tapping his heel and saying, "No, not anymore."

Please, Joseph, how can I make you want me again? And sweetheart, it's not true what you said—about how I always want whatever I can't have. At least I don't think so. I think of you all the time. If you come home, I'll always tell you the truth. Always!

I offered to fix Hetty's hair—that funny looking burned-out gap in back. I did it because you want me to be friends with her, same as Daddy. We sort of are. We talk about lots of things.

I can't tell Hetty it was your idea to leave. It's too humiliating. Are Max and Morgan the only ones who know?

Are you ever coming back? I've got to know! If I want you back bad enough, can I make it happen? Maybe if I concentrate real hard . . .

With sudden energy, Katrinka sat upright. She thought, *a fortuneteller! She'll know the answer!* A rush of childish giddiness made her smile and reach for the pink princess phone on the nightstand.

"Hetty darling," she said, "I think maybe Joseph will come home, but I don't know for sure. I'm going to get my fortune told."

"I wouldn't do that if I were you."

"What's the harm in it? I know a fortuneteller."

"You can't take it seriously," said Hetty. "Promise me you won't."

"Of course I won't. It's just fun. She's a gypsy. I'll believe her if it's what I want to hear."

Hetty wanted nothing to do with gypsies. When her grandmother was a baby, two gypsy women tried to steal her. It all sounded terribly wrong, but Katrinka had made up her mind. Concerned for her safety, Hetty reluctantly agreed to accompany her.

CHAPTER SIX

The gypsy woman greeted them with a heavy accent. Raising one heavily painted eyebrow, she announced, "I am Madame Vadoma."

Katrinka introduced herself, and before turning to the purpose of their appointment, she said, "This is Hetty. She's my attorney."

The discovery about Hetty's profession seemed to startle Madame Vadoma. She closed her eyes and placed her fingertips on her temples. "We have a problem," she said. "I'm afraid the necessary psychic energy is absent. Without it, I cannot perform."

Hetty seemed relieved. "That's quite all right," she said. "I know Duke University decided psychic energy isn't worth studying."

Katrinka raised her voice in alarm. "But I need to know if Joseph's coming back! At least you can tell me that much," she cried, "I brought plenty of money. Will he come if I just want him to bad enough?"

Pressing her temples, Madame Vadoma swirled her skin slowly in little circles over her skull. Her eyelids remained closed. "Hmmm, I see someone tall who cares about you. Ah, yes!" Madame Vadoma's hands quivered artfully while some unseen force appeared to move them.

Katrinka was delighted. "Joseph!" she cried.

"No, I do not see a Joseph," whispered Vadoma. She then feigned surprise as her eyes opened to see Hetty. "Ah, it's you I see!"

Whatever she had in mind next, Madame Vadoma announced it would be free of charge. She raised one eyebrow and whispered hoarsely to Hetty. "This Katrinka, she doesn't need a fortuneteller. She'll believe exactly what she wants." Closing her eyes again, her words of advice came with a hiss. "Tell her she must befriend the future. What she treasures most can bring fulfillment."

Katrinka clapped her hands, delighted with the wisdom she overheard.

On the way home, Katrinka was quiet. She had finished the last two orange cream chocolates after breakfast. Now she needed something else to look forward to. She would consider what Madame Vadoma said. With a little figuring, maybe she could make sense of it. Determined to remember everything, she stared out the car window to think.

Hetty almost ruined everything. And she was wrong about fortunetellers. Madame Vadoma says someone tall cares about me She ought to know, because of her special powers. That must mean Joseph. If she's right, it means he'll be coming home, but I'll have to do my part.

Potato Salad on the Sleeves

Hetty's dreams that night were filled with Madame Vadoma and her jangling jewelry. The next morning she thought about her Duke University comment and hoped it didn't sound too dismissive.

She was still in her bathrobe when someone knocked on the cottage door. Who would come so early in the morning? A shadow fell across the small panes of rippled glass, and Hetty suspected it was Ignatz. She gripped the wrought iron latch and opened the door just a crack. There he stood, with his cap in his hands.

"If you've come for Aunt Freydis . . ." she began.

"No ma'am," said Ignatz, clearing his throat. "Uh, I was wondering . . . can I talk with you, man to man?" He looked into the house as if expecting an invitation to enter. Instead, Hetty joined him out on the porch. The door stood open in case she should need to call Morgan for help. "Yes. What's on your mind?"

"Well, see . . . I've got me a problem. When them thugs at the bakery come after Mrs. Fairburn—" He puffed out his

Madame Vadoma's hands quivered artfully.

cheeks as a substitute for thinking. "It's a real lucky break they didn't see her husband's watch fall out. They run off, and I picked it up.

"After I left I remembered it was still in my uniform pocket. Soon as I could, I hitched a ride back here. But the jacket weren't there. And it ain't nowheres in the house, far as I can see." He rolled his eyes. "I had to wait till they was gone first, to go looking.

"But guess what. Turns out I checked the wrong uniform. The one with the watch musta got sent to the cleaners, on account of the potato salad on the sleeves. I won't have nobody thinking I stole it! 'Specially her ladyship. I gotta put the watch back in her purse real quick, like it used to was. Anyways, I gotta do it before she sees it ain't there."

Morgan came from nowhere to join them. "Come in," he said. "I'll call the cleaners. If they've found it, they'll keep it for us."

Minutes later, he and Ignatz drove to Classy Cleaners to pick up the pocket watch.

The Honest Tear

It had been a week since Katrinka visited the fortuneteller. She spent much of that time thinking about Madame Vadoma's advice.

Gripping a fountain pen, she sat at her dressing table. Her hand hovered over the writing paper, but she was unable to steady it. Closing her eyes, she wondered if Joseph could guess the extent of her suffering since his departure. Even so, with a deep breath, she mustered the courage to begin her letter.

CHAPTER SIX

Dear Joseph,
    I know you don't wish to communicate with me, so I'll keep it real short. I went to the doctor today about all the weight I've gained.
    Please tell me your preference for baby names. I would pick either Joseph, Jr. or Josephine, unless you would rather not.
               Forever yours,
                   Katrinka

She leaned over the letter, and a tear fell on the word *Forever*. The blotter blurred it, because she applied it too fast.

"What if Joseph thinks it's a drop of water I put there on purpose? Well, I don't care," she thought. "It's an honest tear, whether he believes it or not."

When the letter was sealed and sent, she felt emotionally drained and had to stretch out on the bed. The waistband of her skirt felt a little tight. She unbuttoned it in order to think better.

The mirror still reflected her stunning beauty, but her face looked puffy from crying. Even before that appointment with Madame Vadoma, she had needed to apply makeup with special care.

Another problem soon wandered into in her mind.

Why did Ignatz have to come back? It's so irritating that the Morganthals trust him. How can I be sure he won't tell everyone about my part in kidnapping Morgan? If he does, Max might make me leave the gatehouse.

At least he would if it wasn't for the evidence I've got against him. Joseph thinks I already confessed about it. He says nobody's smart enough to get away with lying. Can't he see they're not lies? They're just secrets.

If Joseph understood that, maybe he wouldn't be so angry with me. He would still be here.

Clippings

Hetty opened the sunroom window to let in the fresh scent of grass clippings. Morgan was mowing the front lawn. The rose bush was heavy with pink blossoms. When he stopped to tie it back, a phoebe perched on the wooden handle of the mower. Morgan waited to resume his mowing until after the little bird flitted away. Hetty watched the scene until the kitchen phone rang.

It was Marian. "I hate to worry you," she said, "but my sister-in-law is a real piece of work. She wants whatever she can't have. If she makes up her mind to get something, look out. And with Joseph gone, I just thought I should mention it."

Her voice trailed off, but after a deep breath the rest of it came out. "I know Morgan is above reproach," she said, "but he is a man, after all. And can any man really be trusted?"

"Thank you for your concern," said Hetty. "But it's not a worry I plan to think about. It seems to me when you trust people, they live up to it."

Marian sighed. "That's not my experience. There were so many men in and out of my mother's life, you'd need an abacus to count them."

"I know that influenced you. But think how you loved your stepfather, Joey."

"True," said Marian. "Wonderful Joey. If my mother hadn't locked him out, everything would have been different. But she made him move on."

"Well," said Hetty, "I know you're especially glad to have a brother. What if you and Joseph hadn't found each other?"

"Yes." Marian's voice brightened. "And he's a lot like Joey." She sighed. "I only called to say you can't trust men, and now you've wiped out my entire message. Next thing I know, you'll remind me how much I love your father. I shouldn't have called. Just pretend I didn't." She sounded apologetic.

Hetty laughed. "I know your heart's in the right place."

CHAPTER SIX

"Oh, not really. I should be dusting."

"Dusting what?"

"I don't remember. But if I don't look around, I won't feel guilty about what I'm not dusting. That's what I was busy not doing when Katrinka came over. I was surprised to see her. She was wondering if I'd heard from Joseph. I think she's on the way to your place. Maybe she's already there?"

The conversation ended when Hetty heard Katrinka's Mercedes pull up. It stopped alongside the picket fence. Why didn't she drive closer to the gate, where the path began? She opened her door and stepped out in her pink high-heeled pumps. Some sort of folder was in her hand.

Ever so daintily she tiptoed across the gravel to the lawn. Morgan looked up from his mowing. When Katrinka had his attention, she fell with a little squeal and landed prettily—as if posing for a Nieman-Marcus window display. "Help, help!" she cried.

In a flash, Morgan lifted her petite and graceful frame with ease and carried her to the house. "Oh, silly little me!" she said. "What would I have done without your strong arms?"

Hetty opened the door wide for them to enter. Morgan's cheeks colored, and he placed Katrinka on the couch. His unease was commensurate with the responsibility of arranging her skirt across her shapely limbs.

"Dear me! I mustn't break my ankle," she said. "Not now. Being delicate can be so inconvenient." Katrinka blinked her moist and luminous eyes. Her dimpled cheeks were pink with distress. "You're lucky, Hetty dear. With your height, I doubt if your long bones are as fragile as mine.

"Morgan honey," she said, "I just know your healing hands will make it feel better. Hetty, could you go get us some cool water and a cloth?"

Morgan ran to the kitchen and filled a bowl with water. After delivering the water and a dishrag to Hetty, he went back to mowing the lawn.

When Katrinka was alone with Hetty, she sat up and seemed to forget which ankle had troubled her earlier. "I brought you something," she said. Spreading open the folder, she displayed its contents. "I've been saving these newspaper clippings. But I think they should be yours."

Most of them were articles Hetty had already seen. She picked up one of them by the corner. "That's nice of you," she said. "Thank you."

There were headings like *M. Morganthal Elected to School Board; Morganthal Stock Surges as Morgan M. Takes Helm; Our Pick for Congress: Morgan Morganthal.* Some were the same articles Hetty had saved. But there were also pictures from the society pages and the *Tilly Tells All* gossip column. For years, Tilly titillated her readers with news and pictures of Morgan and Katrinka.

The tattered clipping on the bottom of the assortment was one Hetty remembered well. The day before she and Morgan were married, it appeared on the front page of section B. The heading read: *Heartthrob Morganthal to Wed Total Unknown.* Hetty was considered such a nobody that her name wasn't mentioned at all.

The picture of Morgan took Hetty's breath away. His eyes seemed to look straight at her with a kindly trust. Next to his picture was Katrinka's. A sparkling tiara crowned her veil. She looked regal and triumphant—the way she had expected to appear at their wedding.

The picture opened a distressing memory for Hetty. A time when her heart was breaking. She was helping Katrinka prepare to marry Morgan . . . fastening her wedding dress . . . washing her face and hands with a soft cloth. That was the day they pledged to be friends. But it had been a tentative promise. A promise Katrinka would never keep. Hetty frowned.

There's nothing wrong with her ankle. She should have broken it. That's what she deserved. I wonder if today's little drama went just as she had planned. No, she probably meant to fall in the fishpond so Morgan would give her mouth-to-mouth resuscitation.

Ashamed of her thoughts, Hetty placed a soft pillow on the couch and invited Katrinka to rest a while. She spread a towel under her ankles and, while bathing both of them in cool water, she thought.

Friends. She needs friends. That's the only thing wrong with her. It's her heart that's broken, and I share the blame. How would I cope if I'd been the one to lose Morgan?

The day before their wedding was supposed to happen, there were workmen everywhere. The caterers put up pink and white striped tents for the reception. Floral garlands, ribbons and candle lanterns. I couldn't bear to watch. I felt powerless. There was nothing I could do so I hid in the forest. I lay on a branch and told Hannah all my thoughts. I was longing to look at Morgan one last time . . . even from a distance. I hurt all over with wanting it.

I thought of my family. And the charade I had used to hide my sadness. I was sure they would tell me I was too young to have those feelings, but I couldn't bear to pretend any longer. I couldn't stop sobbing.

Morgan had no way of knowing I was so desperate. I was his sister's little friend, nothing more. Or so I thought.

How could I know he felt the same way? Then he came. It was my desperation that brought him. I thought it couldn't happen. My heart was pounding in my throat. When he looked up through the leaves at me, there was no one else in the world.

I said, "I love you, Morgan. I wish I could marry you, instead."

Katrinka stirred, but she looked peaceful. Hetty put the pan of water away in the kitchen and wondered what she should do next.

I can't fix her broken heart, but I can be a friend. Katrinka needs kindness more than attention. Mother says everyone needs a human touch.

Returning to sit by her, Hetty placed a sympathetic hand on Katrinka's shoulder. In that moment, she saw her face soften with grateful humility. It was a sweet satisfaction, and Hetty felt privileged to evoke such an effect.

Before Phil Wallace died, he had asked to talk with Hetty. He said, *Please love my Katrinka. She can seem artificial, but she's real inside. She's my angel.*

Hetty thought of the many years Katrinka had adored her father . . . how she hungered for his attention. Perhaps her longing would never be satisfied. Would it follow her everywhere? Into all her friendships and associations?

Hetty squeezed her hand. For the moment, Katrinka seemed transformed under the touch of someone who cared. Her large eyes looked sadly docile and eager for forgiveness—as if a wounded angel was inside looking out.

Her ankles felt cold to the touch. As Hetty walked toward the window seat to get the afghan, she glanced back over her shoulder. The creamy smoothness of Katrinka's skin and the graceful perfection of her form stunned her.

While gathering the afghan, Hetty saw Morgan framed in the window. He had mowed the strip of lawn next to Katrinka's car. Now he balanced the mower in the air by its wooden handle. His powerful body moved with perfect control.

She had often seen him put away the mower and other tools in this manner. But this time Hetty saw his broad shoulders and firm muscles from a new perspective. A small cry came from her throat. She tried not to think of the newspaper clipping: Morgan and Katrinka—*The Beautiful Couple*. Hetty gripped the window frame. She couldn't take her eyes off Morgan. The sun reflected off his dark hair, and she could hardly breathe.

CHAPTER SIX

I was the total nobody in the triangle. But Katrinka was the one who lost him?

Morgan stopped and whistled in answer to a cardinal's call. The sound echoed deep into the darkness of the woods. He put down the lawnmower and whistled again.

This time, the echo emerged from a place deep inside Hetty's fears—the dark place where she was hiding Marian's conversation. The echo shouted back with all the ugliness of that warning. Hetty shivered as a chill went up her spine. She couldn't deny the truth of what Marian had said: *He is a man, after all. But she wouldn't think of that. Morgan had chosen her.*

Bell Trouble

Hetty tossed restlessly that night, but she wasn't the only one. At two-thirty in the morning, Freydis felt the sudden desperate need for a pencil and a pad of paper. She couldn't remember why, but was sure it was important to the future of something or other.

She got up to look for it, but forgot what it was she needed. Frightened by her own confusion, she sat up the rest of the night until Hetty found her the next morning, shivering in her nightgown.

When Morgan was ten, he had given a bell to his little sister so she could ring it whenever she needed him in the night. Sometimes Melinda would drop her teddy bear over the side of the crib, or have a bad dream and need Morgan to sing *Found a Peanut*. Remembering how well it worked for Melinda, Morgan bought a bell for Freydis. He and Hetty told her to ring it any time she needed their attention.

Freydis rang it when she was desperate for their help, which was every night.

One time she claimed to have misplaced the moon, and Morgan reassured her by opening the curtains. He smiled and said, "I guess it just went offstage for a while." She was grateful and relieved she hadn't lost the moon permanently.

Then things changed, and the bell rang with greater frequency every night. When asked what she needed, Freydis usually gave the same answer. She would apologize and say she couldn't remember what had been on her mind.

After a few weeks of being exhausted, one night Freydis did remember what was on her mind: her problem was that the bell was keeping her awake. She said, "It keeps ringing all night. And every time I try to sleep, it rings again."

Morgan sympathized. He said, "I have an idea. Would you like me to hide it so it won't keep ringing? That way it won't bother you."

"Oh, thank you, Morgan! Would you?" She squeezed his hand. Freydis was grateful for his wise solution. She slept soundly after that.

The Guest of Honor

Now that the bell no longer disturbed her sleep, Freydis was happy and well rested. And, with the return of Ignatz, she once again took her place in the front seat of the Morganthal limousine.

One day they were on a pleasant and familiar country road and they slowed along a gentle curve. Freydis said, "Oh, Mr. Gorman! What does that sign say?"

"It says, *Haxton Academy Honors Mrs. Fairburn*."

"Are you sure?" Puzzled, she blinked her soft gray eyes.

"Yeah. Your students. And a bunch of folks. They're doing this big thing for you today."

"Oh? Today?"

"Yep. Morganthals is here already." He gave her a broad grin. "But since you asked could I drive, I brung you, which is a distinctive honor."

CHAPTER SIX

"How do I . . . how do I look?" she asked.

"They don't come no prettier than you, ma'am."

"That's kind of you. But truly, Mr. Gorman, there's nothing amiss about my hair?"

"That's how come I took you to the beauty saloon yesterday."

She looked pensive. "My wonderful girls . . . I wonder what I should say to them."

"Well, *you* get to sit real comfortable and hear *other* folks spout off. Leastwise that's what your niece Hetty says. What's the good of being honored, if you gotta work for it?"

"But they all mean so much to me. I must find a way to let them know." She sat up straight and adjusted her shawl.

"I get it. Like the motto, huh? About how you gotta find a way or make one up?"

"That's right," she said. "Inveniam viam aut faciam."

"Man, I shoulda never dropped outa school," said Ignatz. "I ain't never going to talk good like you."

He scowled, and Freydis patted his hand. "My dear friend, I understand you just fine," she said, "and it's never too late for school."

"You think?" said Ignatz. This was a new idea, for sure.

A small group of women and girls stood ahead of them, and he said, "Methinks they're here special to walk you in."

While the welcoming committee mistakenly opened the back door, Ignatz wished her well. "Hope it's a ripsnorter!" he said.

Finding Freydis in the front seat, the committee pinned a corsage on her shoulder and took her to the banquet hall.

Morgan appeared at her side to escort her to the stage, while Hetty held her shawl for safekeeping. From her place at the head table, Freydis saw many people she loved and almost remembered. Leaf and Marian were there. Dan and Dora. Max and Mimi Morganthal. Morgan's sister Melinda and her fiancé Dart Duncan sat at the same table. They must have traveled a great distance.

But where was Mr. Gorman? She searched the faces in the crowd. Turning to the nice lady beside her, she said, "Pardon me, but I don't see Mr. Gorman. Will he be sitting with me?

The Tar Bubble

Ignatz was in the parking lot with sweat trickling down his face. He figured the banquet would take a while, so why not find something to do? The cracks in the hot asphalt were sealed with tar, so he leaned over to inspect a bubble that puffed up.

It oughta be flattened, he reasoned, so he poked the bubble with his finger. Where did the air go? Maybe if he tried another, he'd learn the answer. He did, but this one popped. The pink rag in the trunk didn't clean the tar off his finger. But it worked just fine to wrap it up with, so he wouldn't get tar on things.

Ignatz had his head in the trunk, when he heard a request. "Will you join us inside?"

When he got into the banquet hall, he was planted next to Mrs. Fairburn. Her smile gave him the courage to try the salad in front of him, even though green stuff like that wasn't exactly his kind of food.

The announcer stood up. "I have introduced everyone but Mr. Gorman, who has just joined us at the head table." The gentleman seemed uncertain what further introduction he should make. But he looked at Ignatz long enough that it seemed he was fishing for some response.

Ignatz stood up. This was a real important place, so he chose his words carefully. "Hey, thanks," he replied. He was careful to hide his right hand with the pink rag. "Mrs. Fairburn, she's the main person to which I look up to. That's for sure!" he said.

CHAPTER SIX 135

Did he hear some polite whispering? He sat down quickly. Maybe they were laughing at him! His face was hot, and he hoped it wasn't as red as it felt.

Mrs. Fairburn whispered, "How very thoughtful of you."

Ignatz looked down at his salad. He figured he was pretty much in charge of making it disappear, so he attacked it with his left hand.

Dessert was a bit dainty. He polished off the ice cream on top, while the announcer thanked the Morganthal family for the new sound system. The man said a lot of fancy words about Mrs. Fairburn. That's when Ignatz listened and stopped chewing altogether.

"You have touched so many lives," said the man. "Everyone in this hall today would love to hear your voice." "Would you just say hello?" He handed her the microphone, so she could remain in place.

Freydis slowly opened her purse to find her handkerchief. Was she confused? She said. "I love you all. I remember . . ."

But maybe she didn't remember, because she stopped a while. There were so many people, and they were all smiling their encouragement.

"I came to be your headmistress. I thought, 'I can do this because I love these girls and what they can become . . . what they will become." Her voice was hard to hear. "And I can do this. I can do this . . ." She looked frightened.

Ignatz whispered, "Tell them, you know, how to *find a way or make one.*"

She couldn't hear very well. "I beg your pardon?"

He tried again. "Uh, *In wany wickiam, ad facky outum.*"

Freydis brightened and spoke clearly. "Yes, *I will find a way or make one.* There is such greatness in people. We can do almost anything, if we work at it—and if we know someone believes in us.

"However different we are, words don't separate us, if we listen with our hearts. That's the way we understand.

"I remember the time . . . I remember the time when . . . yes, when John died, and I came to be your headmistress." Freydis reached in her purse and pulled out her husband's pocket watch.

Ignatz forgot about the pink rag. He didn't care if people laughed. He stood up and cheered for his Mrs. Fairburn. Then the Morganthals leapt to their feet, and everyone in the hall followed their example—clapping and blowing kisses.

A swelling of understanding came from hearts that listened. Love was everywhere.

Almost Ready

In two days, Hetty would give a baby shower for Katrinka. She had decorated the invitations with little pressed flowers. Though the process had been time consuming, she felt it was worth the effort.

All but one of the guests had called to accept. Most of them asked what Katrinka might still need. Hetty hadn't the least idea, and it seemed like it would be an invasion of privacy, to ask. She could report only that Katrinka didn't seem to have anything for the nursery yet.

Now the cottage was almost ready for the party. Hetty had bought a new calligraphy pen and a bottle of sepia ink. She worked late into the night to write out the place cards in her best hand. Each place setting had a matching napkin ring with a lace-trimmed napkin.

Pippa watched her mother put the last touches of white paint on a small wicker bassinet that would serve as the centerpiece. On the morning of the shower, Hetty would fill it with fresh flowers from the garden.

Some of the buds Hetty hoped to use were opening too soon, so she had placed umbrellas over them. Now they were sure to bloom at just the right time.

CHAPTER SIX

Pippa said, "Mommy, can we get a baby like Joseph and Trinka?"

"No, but you'll get to see their baby. And you can help me with the party."

"Is the baby coming to the party?"

"Yes, but it's still in Katrinka's tummy."

"Oh . . . " Pippa was thoughtful. "Did she eat it?" Hetty was preparing a long explanation, but Morgan quickly entered to intervene.

As he lifted Pippa high in the air, she asked, "When we get a baby, can I be the mommy?"

"You can be a mommy someday," he whispered, "but I need you for an airplane."

Morgan flew her to the door while Hetty finished painting.

When the brushes were clean and the paints back in storage, Hetty thought of her conversation with Katrinka, ten days earlier.

I expected her to be as excited about her baby as I was. But she said nothing about the future. Why does that disturb me? Maybe she's worried about her waistline. When we were expecting Pippa, Katrinka said I looked like a snake that swallowed a basketball. Could that be on her mind? If only I could share my feelings with her, but I can't. She's not ready to hear them.

Sometimes I watch Morgan and Pippa together and I can hardly contain my happiness—to think I'm a part of their lives. I can hardly believe such trust was placed in me . . . the honor of bearing Morgan's child. I long to feel the first small suggestion of life again—like the flutter of butterfly wings. That's when heaven seemed to whisper secrets . . . to prepare me with strength. And with love for this complicated small person. The memory often comes to me during quiet times.

Hetty looked out the window. Pippa must have touched the wet paint. Morgan wiped her fingers with his handkerchief and then lifted her again to soar toward the back yard.

A change of thought saddened Hetty. How would Katrinka manage if Joseph didn't return to help raise their child?

Hetty and Katrinka were linked by many past experiences that required a degree of forgiveness. But now Hetty felt only sympathy for her. She must do everything possible to help. It felt good to be giving her this shower.

A car pulled up next to the rose arbor. It appeared to be Katrinka. Why would she come here unexpectedly? Hetty wiped her hands on a rag and went to the door.

Good News!

Hetty stepped out onto the front porch to greet Katrinka. The additional fullness of Katrinka's figure contributed to a new radiance. Her large eyes blinked sweetly.

Perhaps it was happiness with her impending motherhood that increased her beauty.

Katrinka glanced at the nest above her in the ivy. "I don't know how you put up with these dirty birds!" she said. The strong scent of perfume preceded her as she entered the cottage.

Hetty indicated the window seat. "Come sit down," she said.

"Oh, you're sweet, but I can't stay! I just came to give you some good news!" She clapped her hands together. "I know you'll be pleased—it's so hard to give a party, with a three-year old getting into everything!

"Anyway, I talked to Mimi last night. I would have called you this morning, but my manicure took absolutely forever! You know how that goes." She inspected her nails, and her pink lips formed a pretty little pout. "Oh, I guess you don't," she said, raising one eyebrow. "You never get your nails done, do you?" She laughed sweetly, and Hetty laughed with her.

CHAPTER SIX

What was her news? Maybe Mimi and Katrinka were getting someone to help her serve the food.

"I'm so relieved I caught you in time," said Katrinka, "before you went to any trouble!" Her dimples came and went with each smile. "I told Mimi I was real worried about you, the way you always try to do too much. I asked if we could have the shower at her house instead, and she said *yes!*"

Katrinka's eyes sparkled with excitement. "You know how *beautifully* she entertains! And she's got everything ready. I've invited Tilly Teller."

She glanced at the little bassinet sitting on newspapers and smiled. "Now you'll have time to paint your little doodad there," she said.

"And don't you worry, honey, I'll call everybody on the guest list and tell them where it's going to be. You *must* come! Maybe we should fix your hair though, in case you show in pictures."

Hetty's mouth went dry. "Yes . . . yes, thank you."

CHAPTER SEVEN

A Heavy Heart

Hetty returned from Katrinka's shower with a heavy heart. The cottage was empty. She sat in the window seat with her head in her hands. The event ran over and over in her mind.

Everyone seemed to feel sorry for me. It was so humiliating! I hate to think what Katrinka said, when she called people. Mimi was kind, as always. But I couldn't tell her what really happened. She would have felt terrible to know I was planning to have the shower here.

Then she asked if I'd play the piano. Mimi meant well, but I felt so close to tears, it would have been a disaster. Should I have done it anyway?

I wanted to look happy for Katrinka. Hard as I tried, I know it didn't work.

This would all go away, if I could confide in Morgan, but I can't. I don't want to look like a whiner. He might think I'm petty and resentful.

I wanted to show him I could entertain. I suppose it hurt my pride. Compared to his mother, I'm so clumsy at doing things.

Mimi knew exactly what kind of party Katrinka would like,

and the caterers served everything beautifully. The soufflé didn't collapse like it would have for me. The table was elegant. Mostly pink. Tilly had plenty to write about in her column.

When Katrinka opened the baby gifts, she didn't seem interested in them. I think the highlight for her was showing everyone Max and Mimi's antique cars. She doesn't seem excited about the baby.

Does she really want it? It's hard enough with two parents. Maybe the thought of raising a child without Joseph is overwhelming right now.

If I had died having Pippa, Morgan could have managed without me. It was hard for him to talk about it, but we both realized it might happen. Mother and Papa were ready to help if they were needed. Father and Marian would have done everything they could, too. Love can make up for whatever is missing.

If Katrinka doesn't want to be a mother, would she let us raise her baby? Maybe she will if Joseph never comes back.

No, I don't suppose she would stand for it. Unless she wants it raised as a Morganthal. How would Morgan feel about it?

I mustn't have such foolish hopes. It's wrong of me to think this way.

Maybe it will be a boy. He'll be three years younger than Pippa. That's the same age difference as there was between Morgan and Katrinka.

Maybe Katrinka will try to be a matchmaker. I can just imagine how it would be. She'll say, "Hetty darling, now that Philippa is eighteen, you need to dress her more fashionably. If only you could interest her in haute couture before she goes to college! My Alphonse obviously deserves a polished and refined wife. You know—more like I would have been for Morgan."

When she pronounces Morgan's name, she'll bat her long eyelashes and pose like the figure on top of a wedding cake.

She'll say, "Couldn't you send her to a finishing school? I can't believe you haven't taught her better. But you wouldn't

CHAPTER SEVEN

know how, you poor thing. She even uses her legs like you do—as if they're just meant for getting around."

Then Katrinka will put her hands on her hips and say, "For heaven's sake! It's an absolute outrage, that's what it is! Such a waste. Everybody knows the whole point in having legs is for the impression they make" She might even threaten to expose one of her shapely limbs as a demonstration.

She'll roll her eyes and say, "The way you and Morgan let Philippa run free and wild, she always has that horrid smell of fresh air. And why do you let her go horseback riding? Last time she rode bareback, her nose got sunburned because you didn't even provide a parasol."

She'll say, "I'm not complaining about all the attention Morgan gives Alphonse. My boy needs to watch a real man in action. He's learning from the best." She'll say it in her you-don't-appreciate-Morgan-as much-as-I-do tone of voice.

I can hear her now. She'll remind me how Alphonse would have been raised in opulent splendor, if Morgan had been his father."

She'll wink at me and say, "You could be enjoying all that beautiful money and fame too, if you had any idea how to handle it! But my real concern is that Philippa doesn't even know to stick out her pinky when she sips from a teacup! But what can you expect, with such poor training, bless her heart."

She'll sigh sweetly and say, "Everyone knows beauty is only skin deep. That's the reason we can see it. Nobody cares about character and brains. They're totally worthless without beauty." For emphasis, maybe Katrinka will pull back her hot-pink lips to flash her gorgeous teeth. Then she'll point to a dimple with her longest pink fingernail.

"My Alphonse is going to be tall like Joseph," she'll say, "and handsome like Morgan. Our two youngsters seem quite fond of each other, but does Philippa have to call him Al? After all, he's fifteen now.

"Hetty darling, in the interest of their future together, I have a plan. I can see your precious Philippa is going to be a skinny, shapeless beanpole like you, with ridiculous hair. So if you don't mind, I'll need to give her a little feminine guidance."

I'll say, "Thank you for your kind but idiotic offer. Actually, Pippa is perfect exactly the way she is. Besides, I prefer that you keep your B-52 hairstyle, or beehive, or whatever it's called, to yourself.

"We realize you don't mind cockroaches living in your hair, even if they should chew through your skull. But I do not want them to take up residence on our daughter's person.

"Perhaps you should get somebody to light your hair on fire, like mine."

Hetty felt the gloom of darkness. It pressed her with a headache, and her teeth bit down on her tongue. Anger had made its own darkness and brought numbness with it. A heavy sadness engulfed her.

There was no feeling in her lips, and she gasped for air. When her breath wouldn't come fast enough or deep enough, the room turned an empty gray and seemed to swirl around her. Had she made the gloom herself?

The sun glared sharply into her eyes, when she opened them. She considered the state of her mind and how it could have created such a sickening misery.

Something has to change. I'm seeing Katrinka with anger and hate. Maybe it's envy. How can I covet her baby? She needs Joseph to come home, and I've been hoping he won't. It's selfish and wrong. I'm thinking all wrong.

Why do I imagine her worse than she is? Maybe it's only natural. When Ignatz came back, Morgan thought he was guilty. It didn't seem at all like him. He never thinks that way. Now I realize it was to protect his family.

CHAPTER SEVEN

Morgan just wanted me to be cautious too. I can't compare that with the way I think of Katrinka. My motives aren't as noble as his. They're just to protect my own feelings, and it isn't working. I feel mostly ashamed. I'm worse than unkind. I'll only hurt myself unless I learn to love Katrinka.

Still . . . I don't want Joseph to come back, or they'll want to raise their baby.

Hetty rearranged the pillows beside her in the window seat. Pippa loved this window when she was tiny—bobbing her head with excitement at the grand outside world. Maybe Katrinka's baby would too.

Music

Leaf got home from the college with a stack of botany exams to correct. He looked around for a place to lay them down, but letters and magazines littered the kitchen counter. Those and several open books suggested Marian had stopped partway through exploring a variety of subjects.

Near the telephone, a few bookmarks poked out *of Silent Spring*. Maybe it would lead to a discussion over dinner. *The Guns of August* and *Hop on Pop* were on top of another pile.

Nothing appeared to be cooking on the stove. But it was still early, and Leaf wasn't hungry yet. He thought if Marian and Danny were away on an errand, he could make dinner before they returned.

A chair was up against the refrigerator. Danny must have stood on it to attach his latest art work. It was a crayon drawing of Hannah. At least it was of some very large and cleverly drawn purple thing that might be a tree.

After wearing a stiff shirt all day, Leaf wanted to change clothes. He wandered to the bedroom and opened the bottom drawer of the dresser. He always put his soft flannel shirts there after he laundered them. His picture of Anne was hiding at the bottom of the stack.

Why did Leaf want a flannel shirt on a warm summer evening? Maybe he didn't. Perhaps he just wanted to see Anne's face. His hands felt under the shirts where he hid the frame. Carefully, he pulled it out and set it on the dresser. Anne looked more like Hetty than he remembered. From where he sat on the bed, he would hardly know the difference between them.

Leaf remembered the day he discovered Hetty dancing in the woods. In his thoughts, he shared the memory with Anne.

I knew who she was the minute I saw her. She had your soft hair and blue eyes. Only twelve years old. She was twirling and singing in the clearing under Hannah. All bones and angles.

The next three years were the hardest . . . secretly watching over her, wanting to be her father. I didn't dare declare myself. I thought it would be unfair to Dan and Dora. We all belong together and always did. I know that now.

Leaf hummed and walked to the window. Marian and Danny were under the cherry tree in the back yard. The bright copper of Danny's hair seemed all the brighter next to his mother, as if he borrowed light from her. They were reading a book with their heads together. Danny jumped up to inspect some small detail of nature before returning to her lap. Whatever Marian's interests, she shared them with Danny. Leaf admired her flair for inspiring their son. She seemed to sense the best approach for his level.

The scene gave Leaf such satisfaction that he almost forgot Anne's picture. When he returned to the dresser, he was confident Anne would not resent his neglect. She was there for him as always. But she didn't speak to his mind—probably because he was thinking about dinner. Maybe lamb chops and asparagus?

With his left hand holding the picture frame, he prepared to replace it under the shirts. But first he wanted to just touch the glass over her cheek. As he did, the melody he had been

CHAPTER SEVEN

humming returned to play in his head. Samuel Barber's *Adagio*. A sudden nostalgia gripped him, and he looked at her eyes.

That was our song, Anne, but you never got to hear it. Toscanini conducted it. It was the November after you died. I was out of the hospital and almost over my depression. The Adagio was too beautiful to turn off, so I listened to it often. It consoled me. Or maybe it tortured me. I'm not sure which.

I would have been with you when you died if I'd even dreamed it could happen. Why didn't you tell me how dangerous your pregnancy was? Somehow Freydis and John helped me muddle through your funeral. I remember the shock of seeing you in the casket, but the rest is just a blur.

You just knew the fires were bad and the Forest Service needed me. But you should have asked me to come home. That last fire left me oddly bewildered. Reason told me I wasn't responsible for Zack's death, but the nightmare never left me.

What could I have done differently? It had to be either Zack or Dan—I couldn't have revived them both. If I'd found Zack first, Dan would have died.

Fighting fires with Dan and Zack . . . the three of us had so many good times. It was only that last experience that shook me, when I couldn't save Zack. Dan doesn't talk about it either.

I didn't know if Hetty survived, but I knew Dan and Dora would be good parents. I'll be forever indebted to them. To them and to Marian.

I just wish you could know Marian. She seems to have a sixth sense where Hetty's concerned. She's sure something's troubling Hetty. She's always right.

I hope a music night with the family can help cheer her up. We used to do it more often when Freydis could accompany us. Hetty and I are working on a duet. And we're fiddling around with some western and bluegrass to accompany Marian's yodeling.

Leaf Locke would do anything possible for his daughter's happiness, and Marian was a wholehearted partner in that endeavor. It was Hetty who had brought them together, for which they were most grateful.

Holding the frame in both hands, Leaf felt Anne's eyes looked back at him with love—and sincere approval of his partnership with Marian. He glanced out the window at his young redheaded wife, put the picture back in place, and closed the drawer. He smiled and hummed. It was the same melody as before, but without the accompanying sadness.

Marian had a positive outlook. She was often the glue that kept him together. She understood some of Leaf's memories were hard to dispel; however, she didn't believe in crying over spilled milk.

Lamb chops and asparagus, he thought, *and maybe a chiffon pie? If I sweep the patio, we could eat in the back yard.*

He and Marian kept different things glued together. The arrangement couldn't be more satisfactory.

I Watch Him

The next morning, Marian was absorbed in reading her new book when a knock came at the laundry room door. She tucked a sock in page ninety-two, before laying it on the table. Who could be coming to the back entrance?

"Joseph! Is it possible?" she said. "It's only been two weeks! I thought you were never coming back."

"Sorry to pop in this way, Sis." He laughed and lifted her off her feet.

Marian took him by the hand, past the pile of laundry, to sit at the kitchen table. In no time, he was tipping back his chair in his usual good-natured way, grinning and chuckling. "Katrinka doesn't know I'm back," he said. "Can I hang out with you till the florist opens?"

Marian nodded. "Of course. Tell me what's going on."

He tucked his thumbs in his belt. "Change of plans, you could say. Major change. Tomorrow I meet with Max and

Morgan. We've got to figure out what's next." He seemed to look through Marian. "I feel useless in Africa," he said. "Morgan was right to think it was a hasty decision. All I can do is swat mosquitos and watch poachers kill the elephants. I can't stand what's happening. But Africa can't solve the elephant problem in the foreseeable future." He shook his head.

Marian leaned forward. "Oh, so this isn't about the baby?"

Joseph grinned and drummed the table. "Ah hah! You know. So she's telling people now? Just four more months to go!" he said. "I didn't bring it up, in case Trink wouldn't want me to."

"Everyone knows," said Marian. "In fact I went to a shower for her yesterday. It was supposed to be at the cottage, but Katrinka called at the last minute and said Hetty couldn't manage it. They had to move it to Mimi's."

"That's nice of Mimi," said Joseph. He looked thoughtful. The faucet was dripping on a stack of dishes, and he turned his attention to it for a moment.

His smile faded. "Katrinka is focused on the past," he said. "I feel like she still belongs to her father and Morgan, but not to me."

"You'll work it out," said Marian. She spoke quietly. "I know what it feels like to share someone you love. I used to resent it. But now I don't need Leaf to stop caring about Anne. Not anymore. She'll never be really dead to him," she said. "I get it now, and it's okay. In fact, maybe his feelings for me are deeper because he loves her too.

"Give her some time, Joseph. Whatever Katrinka admired in her father and Morgan, she'll come to appreciate those same qualities in you."

Joseph rocked back in his chair. "In case you think I'm jealous—I'm not."

Marian tilted her head and gave him a crooked little smile.

"Okay, so maybe I am!" He slapped his knees and laughed.

"Still, it's no fault of Morgan's. He's a good friend. One way or the other, he'll always affect both Katrinka and me. I want to learn, so I watch him."

Joseph rolled up his sleeves to wash the dishes. "I've got fifteen minutes, and then I'm off to get pink roses."

A New Start

Joseph stood looking at Katrinka, holding the roses in his hands.

She blushed. "I didn't expect to see you again," she said.

Her hands gripped the table behind her. Gone was Phil's small furniture. She had replaced it with a set that was more suitable for Joseph.

He glanced at the table, so she had to change her answer. "I mean I didn't know for sure if I would."

He laughed. "Yes, you did."

While Katrinka's fingers explored the edge of the table, Joseph appeared to look for something special in her eyes, but she seemed guarded.

He shifted his weight. "I got your letter," he said.

Striding to the sink, he ran cold water over the stems of the roses. Maybe doing something with the flowers could fill the uneasy time—at least until one of them knew what should happen next.

Joseph looked over his shoulder and grinned. "These are for you, Trink."

She was still locked to the table. "Aren't they for the baby, like everything else? That's why you came back."

Joseph dried his hands. "We'll make a new start," he said. "I want to be here for you."

"I . . . I should go to the office," she said. She moved uncertainly toward the box of keys on the hall table.

Over the key box hung a large mirror that had reflected her image with regularity. For years, she had primped and preened in front of it while admiring herself from all angles. But this time, her luminous eyes were on Joseph.

Perhaps she expected the angle of the mirror to make her happiness less obvious, but it did not. Her joy and eagerness were transparent. She seemed to soak in everything about him.

Her fingers fumbled for the car keys while she watched his reflection.

Joseph was not one to hang his hopes on senseless dreams, but he had been looking for something in her countenance, and he found it now. Not once did Katrinka show an interest in her own reflection.

"The flowers are beautiful," she said. Her hand remained in the key box, sifting through it absently. When Joseph approached her from behind, her eyes softened and her cheeks became quite flushed with excitement.

Just to be sure of what he was seeing, he stood quietly for a moment, until a new assurance swelled within him.

This is a complicated woman, he thought, *but now she's mine.*

He took her hand and slowly closed the key box.

The Boiling Point

Morgan knew Joseph could use some time with Katrinka, so he and his father put off meeting with him about the elephant project.

Rather than telling Hetty about Joseph's return, Morgan thought it would be more fun to surprise her. It would do Hetty good to see the cheerful Joseph. When the day came for Morgan to meet with him, Hetty had some documents to prepare at the office, so the two of them drove there together.

Soon after they arrived at the office, Katrinka made a grand entrance, swishing through the door in a loose, flowing dress. Its pastel colors complemented her radiant complexion.

When Joseph came in close behind her, Morgan saw something that surprised and worried him. At the sight of Joseph, Hetty appeared disturbed. She turned pale, and her speech was halting.

All the while, Katrinka's face glowed with pleasure. She winked and fanned her lovely, long artificial eyelashes. "I'll be giving my darling husband as many babies as he wants," she cooed. She fingered the pink silk flowers surrounding the sweetheart neckline of her dress. Gazing at Hetty, she raised her chin as if to highlight her superior maternal situation.

Morgan glowered at Katrinka's insensitivity, but Hetty recovered her composure and smiled. "Wonderful!" she said. "I'm glad to see you both so happy."

"Hetty honey," said Katrinka, "could we talk? I'm heading to a press conference. I haven't told you about my new ad campaign."

They disappeared into Hetty's office, leaving Morgan and Joseph to wait for Max.

Morgan was puzzled. What had Joseph done to upset Hetty? Maybe he was as unfeeling as Katrinka. How could he just stand there and let his wife gloat about the bushels of babies she could have? As if it was the easiest thing in the world.

I can't stand his self-satisfied look, thought Morgan.

Hetty had made an effort to celebrate Katrinka's good fortune. Always with generous kindness, in spite of her sorrow. Morgan wondered why she never turned to him for comfort. It seemed as if she no longer needed him for her happiness.

Dora Lawrence arrived with a batch of oatmeal cookies and sat at her desk. Morgan's mood became dark as he listened to his mother-in-law and Joseph in conversation. While Joseph and Dora talked, Morgan felt his fury rise with Joseph's unbearable cheerfulness.

He remembered what Marian had said: Joseph didn't want Hetty to befriend Katrinka. What kind of mean-spirited scum would have such an attitude! She would do anything to help them, and Morgan wanted to defend her. How could Joseph reject Hetty's friendship so rudely?

Just then, Joseph threw back his head and laughed. Slapping his thigh, he said something about Father's Day. He had no right to be so carefree!

Morgan scowled and clenched his fist. In anger, eyes glaring under his heavy brow, he faced Joseph. *Stop that!* he thought. Deep inside, he seethed with explosive energy, intending to grab Joseph by the collar. The muscles of his neck tightened, and he raised his fist.

Joseph's eyes widened with startled confusion. Morgan was his friend—the man he most admired. Though Joseph was taller, few men could match Morgan's power.

Suddenly sickened by memories of his father's early violence, Morgan relaxed his fist. He alone knew how close he had come to attacking Joseph. Their friendship was more important than any ill feelings. Hetty's gentle influence had brought harmony to him and his family. He mustn't do anything to spoil it.

Morgan flashed a broad smile at his friend. "Happy Father's Day, Joseph."

It was an apology, and Joseph knew it.

Bless Her Heart

Katrinka left Hetty's office and drove toward the LuvCon offices. She checked her watch. She was already late. The press conference was supposed to start ten minutes ago.

The speed limit was ridiculously low; however, Katrinka didn't want to get caught speeding. She had been in trouble twice for inventing a story about a broken speedometer.

Her conversation with Hetty had taken longer than it should have. But what choice did she have? Madame Vadoma had correctly predicted Joseph's return, so she had to bring that to Hetty's attention. Fortunetellers obviously had special powers after all.

Katrinka knew what she said about having lots of babies probably hurt Hetty. But it couldn't be helped. It had been such an obvious thing to say. Still, she blushed to think it might have sounded rude.

Suddenly, Katrinka's thoughts shifted to a serious worry, and her pretty pink lips formed a frown.

I don't know what to do. If I get up the nerve, Hetty's the only person I can tell about the trouble I'm headed for. I don't know how to go about it, but I think I'll need her help. I can't go on this way.

Worry would accomplish nothing. Katrinka forced herself to snap out of it and concentrate on the press conference.

This is the first time when Hetty won't be with me. But she'll get to see it all in the newspaper. We can talk about it later.

I think my new slogan sounded good to her. "When Beauty Calls, Love Answers."

I like it better all the time. It's going to be a good year. Hetty thinks if anyone can make it work, I can.

A peculiar thought crossed Katrinka's mind. Should she tell Joseph how nice Hetty was while he was gone? No. It would be of no benefit to her, so she dismissed the idea. Still, it felt good to think Hetty was a friend, whether she could resolve anything or not.

Something was happening in front of the office, so Katrinka parked in back to avoid the commotion. Checking the arsenal of beauty products in her bag, she locked the car and hurried through the rear entrance.

Hetty had been quite complimentary when she saw Katrinka's dress. Maybe she liked the full-figured look because she couldn't obtain it herself. But Katrinka didn't want to look large and shapeless. In case her admirers had higher expectations, she would make some quick changes.

In her dressing room, she selected a lavender sash and used it to cinch in the waist of her dress. She sucked in her stomach, but the sash was already as tight as she could stand

CHAPTER SEVEN

it. A long silk scarf added just the right touch. After wrapping it once around her neck, she let it flow downward to cover as much as possible.

One more look in the mirror, and Katrinka felt better. She thought, *according to Hetty, the reason Daddy loved me wasn't just because I'm beautiful.* She tilted her head. *But I'm not sure he would have, if I'd been ugly.*

She sighed. *Daddy wouldn't approve of how I got Joseph to come home.*

Again she thought of her new slogan: *When Beauty Calls, Love Answers.* Her perfect little pearly white teeth showed in a smile. Moistening her lips, she breathed deeply with the exhilaration of success.

Before proceeding, Katrinka made sure everything was ready for the unveiling.

An assistant had arranged her signature pink and white striped bunting around the platform. This time, the presentation should be exceptionally thrilling. The design of the new compacts and magnifying mirrors; the latest lipstick colors; the crystal perfume bottles—all of it would meet with a standing ovation. It always did.

The new *Katrinka* perfume had been through many expensive and risky trials. The whole process would always remain secret. The less Hetty knew, the happier Katrinka would be. Hetty would insist on having LuvCon be open and forthright about what was going on in the labs. Even Katrinka felt rather uncomfortable with their animal testing so she made sure Hetty didn't know about it.

Stepping into the spotlight, Katrinka took the microphone. But before she spoke, restless whispers from the audience signaled something was wrong.

A strident voice called out, "Why did you lie about animal testing?"

The man behind him cried out, "Yeah, what's going on!"

To either side of them, a surly belligerence spread like waves, but Katrinka's eyes were shining. This was her opportunity to blend personal charm with diplomacy.

Abandoning her prepared text, she flounced gracefully into the audience and said, "More than anyone I know, you special, special people deserve the truth! Truth and beauty are at the core of *everything* we do here at LuvCon. It's always been that way."

Her perfume wafted magically through the group, calming them like smoke over a swarm of bees. Dreamily, she whispered into the microphone, "Your trust is such a beautiful thing! It would absolutely break my heart to lose it."

Everyone within hearing appeared eager to prevent such a tragedy. If she had lost control of the procedure, no one knew it.

A swarthy man on the aisle, touched by her lovely and sincere honesty, blushed and took up his pencil. His expression relaxed as her graceful hands caressed the back of his chair.

Throughout the questions and answers, the picketers outdoors chanted and shrieked, over and over, "They have no voice—they have no choice!"

But Katrinka ruled. The deliciously unfiltered answers that flowed from her sweet lips captivated the entire room.

"I'm sure my attorney felt confident no one would investigate," she said, "so she advised me not to say anything about the testing. But she's so *darling,* I know she'll want to take full responsibility for all of it." Katrinka's dimples flashed with the word "darling."

A man with tiny, sunken eyes raised his hand. "Are you talking about the lawyer Hetty Morganthal?" he asked.

Katrinka posed gracefully under the lights. She laughed in such a disarming way that all eyes turned to her as she had hoped. "Yes, I am!" she said.

With those three little words, she implied his question was so clever and delightful that she was thrilled and honored to be under the same roof with such a brilliant mind.

You special, special people deserve the truth!

He followed with another question. "Then why isn't she here?"

Katrinka winked and said with a sweet, endearing giggle, "Well, would *you* be?"

The laughter that followed drowned out the picketers. She waited to regain their attention.

"So, my attorney made a silly little slip," she said. "Bless her heart, can't we allow her a little bad judgment once in a while?"

Public Rebuke

After having talked with Katrinka at the office, Hetty finished her work and left for home. Her father and Marian had spent the morning there at the cottage with Pippa. Leaf was sure to exaggerate his granddaughter's perfection. Both Hetty and Morgan loved him for it, and there was no one to discourage the practice.

While driving, Hetty listened to the local radio station. At first she was only vaguely aware of Tilly Teller's voice. But when she heard Tilly mention animal rights picketers at LuvCon, she gave the broadcast her full attention.

Hetty was stunned by what she heard.

"The public wonders if Morgan Morganthal is suffering from troubles at home," said Tilly. "He has always run a tight ship, so to speak. But maybe he's losing his grip. Otherwise, why is a man of such influence unable to rein in his wife?"

Hetty's fingers tightened on the steering wheel as she listened for more.

Tilly spoke with excitement. "LuvCon Cosmetics has become a profitable arm of the Morganthal business empire—and the jewel of our city. The person most responsible for the current success of LuvCon is the well-known beauty queen and CEO of the company, Katrinka Wallace." Tilly's words were smooth as honey. "Miss Wallace has refused to test her beauty products on innocent animals," she said. "However, it seems her attorney advised her to do it anyway. Then she had Miss Wallace deny it!

"Hetty Morganthal is that attorney. Mark my words, we have to wonder if Hetty Morganthal may have *intended* to tarnish Katrinka Wallace's image.

"Of course, we can only *guess* why the wife of Morgan Morganthal might give shady legal advice to Katrinka Wallace. I would never make any accusations until I know more. You know that. But you be the judge."

Hetty's face was hot, and her eyes stared straight ahead. She stopped the car by the side of the road to listen.

"You see," Tilly added gleefully, "the beautiful Katrinka Wallace was once the fiancée of—yes, you guessed it— Morgan 'Heart-throb' Morganthal!

"Miss Wallace may soon deserve our sympathy," said Tilly. "Think of the difficult position this could put her in. All because of the jealous wife of her former fiancé, who happens to be her boss.

"Mind you," said Tilly, "Miss Wallace graciously asked the public to forgive attorney Morganthal.

"But don't you think the man with the power should take the responsibility?" She clucked her tongue in rebuke. "I believe I can speak on behalf of the state and our community. I predict, when the dust settles, we'll be saying, 'Shame on you, Morgan Morganthal!'"

Rage and humiliation gripped Hetty. Clutching the knob, she killed the horrid voice with an angry snap of her wrist and addressed the silence with clenched teeth.

CHAPTER EIGHT

The Reluctant Advisor

After meeting with his father about the clown partnership, Morgan had a lot of thinking to do. He hiked to a place he had often visited over the years. Following a narrow path worn by many woodland creatures, he arrived at the river's edge.

Gathering a few flat pebbles for his pocket, Morgan walked downstream to a large rock that extended over the water. A cluster of ferns nodded their fiddleheads over the bank. Sometimes he and Hetty sat on this rock. They would lean their backs together while Pippa tossed sticks into the river. With hushed voices, they did little to disturb the quiet rippling of the water. And they took special care to leave the ferns untouched.

Morgan sat on the rock and watched the water striders. The little insects seemed to skate on the surface of the water without effort.

If only everything could be as easy as that, he thought. He decided it would be a shame to disrupt them by skipping rocks across the river.

He was deep in thought when a sweet, melodic voice broke the silence. "My, my, look who's here!"

It was Katrinka. She tossed her hair and posed at the edge of the rock. Her lips formed a little rosebud then parted sweetly, in full-bloom.

"Who told you where I was?" he asked.

"Nobody. I knew this was your thinking place." The sharp heel of her pink pumps mashed a fragile fiddlehead. Her laugh was like the tinkling of little bells. "I used to follow you here and watch you skipping rocks. But you knew that."

Morgan's face colored. "No, I didn't."

"Don't be modest, Honeybun. I'm not the *only* girl who followed you."

Morgan stared at the water. "Why did you come?" It was not so much a question as a complaint, and he didn't wait for the answer. "I was just leaving," he said.

"But why? You just got here, sweetheart."

He turned away. "Being here like this—it's no good."

She pouted. "If you don't want to be alone with me, just say so!"

"I don't."

"Morgan Morganthal! Why can't you see your appeal? Your magnetism!" She appeared ready to faint dramatically at any moment, with the romantic tragedy of it all. Her long eyelashes languidly fanned the air, but Morgan wasn't watching.

"Don't," said Morgan.

Katrinka stiffened. "Do you have to make such a kerfuffle about it?"

Moistening her pretty pink lips, she adjusted her hair to look especially alluring.

"Kerfuffle?" Morgan chuckled with amusement.

Katrinka tried a new approach. "We're just old friends," she said sweetly.

He walked toward the path. "Right," he said. "With a history."

She followed him. "Please don't go! You asked me why I'm here," she said. "It's because . . . well, I need advice."

CHAPTER EIGHT

Morgan detected an unexpected humility. He paused and looked behind him. If she needed his thoughts concerning the business, she would have to follow him. He was leaving.

"Please," she whispered, "Tell me . . . I thought I knew what men wanted. Is there something wrong with me?"

"Wrong with you?"

"Yes." Her eyes were moist with distress. "I thought it would be easy," she said, "if I just married the right man."

Morgan stared across the river. Perhaps he could locate some helpful distraction to rescue him from this conversation.

"So why doesn't Joseph love me?"

Morgan hesitated briefly. "It's all well and good to marry the right person," he said, "but it's even better to *be* the right person."

"No, I mean really, Morgan," she said. "People can't just turn into somebody they're not."

This discussion was unsettling, and Morgan clenched his jaw.

Katrinka began again. "I know you never wanted to marry me. It was our fathers, wasn't it? Max and Daddy planned the whole thing!"

He frowned and started along the path again. "I need to go, Trink."

There was desperation in her voice. "When Hetty got Ignatz to kidnap you, I was sure it would backfire. But no, she went around looking all dewy-eyed and innocent. Hetty was too clever!" Katrinka's voice was shrill. "If it hadn't been for her, you and I would have been real happy together."

She paused to regain her self-control. "Would it have helped if I'd ever gone up in the glider with you?"

This had become unpleasantly complicated. "No," he said.

"Then tell me," she said, "what does Hetty have that I don't? First it was you. Now Joseph. She's not as pretty as me, but it's like I lose out or keep getting her leftovers."

"No, Joseph's a fine man. You should be proud to take his name."

"But why is Hetty everybody's ideal? Tell me! I can take the truth."

Morgan turned around. "The truth? Okay, let's talk about *truth*." His dark eyes were fixed on her.

She squirmed and her cheeks colored. "Morgan honey, I can explain about the press conference! We do whatever we have to, for LuvCon, don't we?" She winked sweetly. "And of course Tilly kind of exaggerates when she gets on the radio."

"Press conference?" he said. "I don't know anything about that."

"Oh!" Katrinka was visibly relieved. "Well anyway, if you'd heard the questions, you'd see why I didn't have any choice."

"There's always a choice," he said. "Always. Figure that out, and you've got the point of life."

He returned to their earlier topic. "About what men want—like everyone else, they want the truth. Or you lose trust."

"But I'm afraid Joseph won't love me if I tell him the truth about some things."

"So you lie to make him love you?"

"Don't make fun of me, Morgan!"

"Sorry, Trink. I care about you. But I won't do marital advice."

She was panting to keep up. "Then how can I make him happy? *Someone* must know!"

He stopped and leaned over to tie his left shoe. "That would be Hetty," he said.

Katrinka was panting. Looking down at the path, she blinked to control her tears. "Joseph says he doesn't care if I get wrinkles, but I know he can't mean it!" she sniffed. "He says the same as you. He just wants me to be honest."

"So, are you?"

She started to cry. "*Of course* I am!" she said. "So, what do I do now? Should I be even *more* honest with him?"

"More?" Morgan chuckled and flashed a smile. "Think how that sounds. Either you are or you aren't."

CHAPTER EIGHT

"I sort of am. I mean I have to be myself. It's just the way I am. I can't help it."

Morgan raised his eyebrows. "Can't you? It's a choice."

Katrinka stared at him. "Maybe I'm not good enough for Joseph any more. Hetty's the only person who would know if I am. But how can I talk to her? I'll always play second fiddle to Hetty."

"No, Katrinka. Just a different fiddle."

Morgan glanced at his watch, hoping it might look like someone was waiting for him somewhere. Anywhere.

Katrinka sobbed. "But maybe Hetty hates me, after all the things I've done to her."

Morgan could think of no appropriate way to console her. In case privacy would help, he turned his back to her.

Rather than appear unsympathetic, he soon faced her again. "Hetty doesn't do hate," he said. "She's better at love."

"Oh Morgan, I'm so afraid! I've been bad forever, and you don't know the half of it. Neither does Joseph." Her voice trembled.

"And I was mean to my mother. But what could I do? I was afraid I'd grow up to look ugly, like her. I couldn't help it," she whimpered.

Katrinka's eyes widened. This time she mouthed her words. "I ... I couldn't help it."

After a long silence, she said, "That is, I meant . . ." Her voice trailed off, leaving only the sound of rippling water and the rustle of wind in the trees. Her countenance reflected a new understanding, as if she saw the foolishness of her statement.

One of her eyelashes drooped from the corner of her eyelid, and her shoulders slumped. Morgan saw the Katrinka he had once known—his dear childhood friend and playmate. She sniffled. Her lip quivered, and a tear rolled down her cheek.

There was something lovely and real about her, and she needed him.

Something You Should Know

Intense energy controlled Hetty on the drive home, and her head rang with Tilly Teller's accusations.

Yet a drab confusion of emotions seemed to blur boundaries. The lines were gone between beauty and ugliness. There was no pleasure. No pain. The reflection in the car mirror told Hetty she was normal, but she had to touch her face. *Is this what hate feels like? There's nothing inside me.*

Staring at the cottage, she wondered how she could go in. *Katrinka stole my feelings,* she thought. *Am I broken? I don't know if I can love anymore. Can I even love Morgan?*

Her car stopped at the rose trellis. For the first time, she saw how insects defiled the roses, crawling in and out of them without apology. But she didn't care. The beetle traps were pregnant with rotting Japanese beetles. Noxious weeds threatened to choke the creeping phlox.

Like wooden stumps, Hetty's uncertain legs carried her to the hammock. Until she could face the family, she would have to lie there and work things out. Maybe Morgan was already here at home. Whether he was or not, she wondered if she should plan some explanation.

No, that's what Katrinka would do, she thought. What's the matter with me? I'll just tell him the truth. If he goes past LuvCon on the way home, he'll see the picketers. He'll know I didn't tell Katrinka to lie. Or will he?

Why didn't I go to the press conference when Katrinka told me about it? Morgan would have, if it had been his responsibility. I'm in over my head, but he won't say so. His kindness hurts too much. That's the worst thing of all. I don't want to see him.

Oh, Morgan, I'm so sorry! I mustn't hold onto this ugliness. I need to get over it. I know I can, if I think of you.

Don't forgive me, Morgan. Just be angry. I understand anger now.

CHAPTER EIGHT

The tears came. Hetty gripped a low-hanging branch to push and pull the hammock, hiding her face behind its leaves.

This is the branch I meant to prune, she thought. But maybe it's all right that I didn't get around to it. Pippa might look out the window, and I don't want her to see me. She'd want me to sing with her before her nap.

The regular back and forth rocking rhythm of the hammock should have been soothing. Hetty wanted to remember lying there next to Morgan. But when she pulled the branch closer, it snapped like one of Hannah's brittle branches. Her lips tightened. The magnificent oak tree didn't have long to live, and Hetty couldn't stand to think about it.

She closed her eyes. Gentle thoughts of Morgan had always brought her a perfect brightness of hope. But this time she couldn't remember the light they shared. Maybe she was expecting too much. How could such memories come on the heels of her murky thoughts?

If I'm in over my head, I need to start swimming. I've been flailing around too long, but I refuse to sink. I just need to decide what shore to swim to.

Why did I ever think I might raise Katrinka's baby? What a ridiculous dream! I need to be happy for her, instead. They'll both need friends. Maybe we can help them together.

I refuse to be an object of pity, like the cardinal we saw at the fishpond. All day long it gathered food to feed the fishes. Father said it was because it didn't have young of its own. Cardinals have such a strong mothering instinct they'll feed anything with an open mouth.

Hetty opened her eyes to a bright patch of sky framed in lacy foliage. For a fleeting moment, a kestrel soared and hovered in the space directly above her. She knew a little about kestrels. It made her smile to remember the female was longer than the male.

Within seconds, the graceful bird left for someone else's patch of blue, but Hetty kept the memory of it. She thought of the kestrels' well-known boldness. *That's what I'll have to be—a kestrel! And I'll fly facing the wind.*

Things were starting to come together, until trouble crept into her mind. She gasped. *How can I handle my next radio show? This Saturday, my guest is Tilly Teller.*

I'll face the wind, that's how. Morgan shouldn't have to prop me up whenever I have a problem or disappointment. He's the one I don't want to disappoint.

I want to deserve you, Morgan, and I will. Boldly! Why have I been so been blind? I know where I want to end up. Always close to you.

The crunch of gravel signaled an approaching car. It was Katrinka's Mercedes. Oddly, she was in the passenger seat, and Morgan was driving.

Hetty didn't want to be seen looking lazy, when there was so much to do. They might discover her, and she hadn't even gone inside to see Pippa.

Katrinka waited for Morgan to open her door then put out her hand for his support. The two of them spoke quietly for a moment.

Apparently Hetty wasn't as invisible as she had hoped. "There she is," said Katrinka.

Then Morgan called out, "Hetty, Katrinka needs to talk with you."

"I'll leave," said Morgan. "You tell her." Katrinka embraced him, and he started for the back yard.

Was there something Morgan didn't want to say? Hetty stood up quickly. Her face turned white, and she crumpled to the ground in a faint.

When Hetty's eyes blinked open, Katrinka was standing over her in a posture of dominance. A suggestion of pleasure formed on Katrinka's glossy lips. Maybe seeing their embrace caused Hetty to faint. She appeared to find satisfaction in that possibility.

With an artificial pink smile, Katrinka showed her gleaming row of teeth. "What's wrong, honey?" she purred.

"I'm here because, Morgan and I . . . that is, we decided there's something you should know."

A Day to Remember

Earlier that morning, Ignatz received a call from Hetty Morganthal. She hoped he wouldn't mind picking up Mrs. Fairburn sooner than they had planned. She said, "For some reason, Aunt Freydis got ready at six o'clock this morning."

When he arrived at the cottage, Mrs. Fairburn was waiting for him under the rose trellis. She sat straight, holding a small package in her white-gloved hands. The veil of her hat was up, and he could see the light of excitement in her gentle gray eyes.

Doffing his cap, he said, "Oh, ho! So we're delivering a package today, are we?"

"Yes, but I can't think how I planned to do it."

Ignatz thought maybe she had forgotten more than that. "Want me to check who it's for?"

She smiled like a real grandma. "Not yet, thank you."

"Well," he said, "when you give the say-so, it'll help me get a idea where we gotta drive to."

"It won't matter, Mr. Gorman."

As she read the card and fingered the ribbon, her face glowed with pleasure.

"My handwriting is a little shaky," she said. "I can hardly read it myself. But I can tell you what it was meant to say."

Her knowing smile intrigued Ignatz. "Like what, I prithee?" he asked.

She made no answer, but opened the card repeatedly. It seemed to amuse her.

"Just thinkin'," he said. "I ain't never seen you come out with a real belly laugh. That some kinda rule for ladies?"

"What are you saying, Mr. Gorman? I wouldn't be a good Santa Claus?"

"No ma'am!" Then hoping not to offend her, he said, "I mean you get to be whoever you want!" He was unable to stop laughing, and it seemed to delight her.

"Dear Mr. Gorman, you laugh quite well enough for the two of us."

Free of care, they rode along the country roads until Ignatz asked if she might tell him the time. She reached in her purse for John Fairburn's pocket watch.

Where could it be? She took off her right glove to explore the inner recesses of her handbag. Then the light dawned. "Oh, my!" she said. "I've played a trick on myself." Though quiet and restrained, the unmistakable sound of laughter came from someplace inside Mrs. Fairburn.

Before her recovery, she said, "I have something for you." The package was for him.

"Me, you say?" His hands shook as he unfolded the card. Her handwriting was too hard to decipher, but she promised it had his name on it.

"Now you will always be on time for class," she said. She smiled at him like he really belonged in this experience.

He would always remember the way she said it. But did he dare believe her words?

It was her husband's pocket watch. "Oh, man!" His head wobbled with emotion.

What was he supposed to say! There must be rules for this kind of thing. "I ain't letting it out of my sight," he said. "Him being dead and all—you sure your husband don't mind? I mean he won't roll over, will he?"

"No, he's proud of you, too." She puzzled briefly over what she heard herself say. "That is I'm sure he would be," she said. "He knows you can do it. But I'm afraid John Fairburn passed away."

The watch was more elegant than he remembered.

CHAPTER EIGHT

Hours passed, and Ignatz was happy keeping track of the time until he returned to the Morganthal estate. When he arrived, Max was holding his driving cap and waiting for him. "Ignatz, bring the Duesy around front."

"What? You mean, like drive it?" He would have dropped his teeth, if they weren't attached.

"How else?" said Max. "And put the top down."

Ignatz checked his appearance in the mirror and straightened his tie.

Just for practice, he removed the watch from his trouser pocket and slipped it back in. He hadn't noticed the small pocket before, but Mrs. Fairburn told him men's pants always had a special one for watches. She knew just about everything there was to know.

Just a quick once-over with the feather duster, and the car was ready to go. Ignatz had lowered the canvas top earlier, just because it wasn't against the rules. He dusted the gleaming exhaust pipes that extended through the side panels of the hood.

Her cream-colored body was enough to make a man drool. He pulled her forward, slow and easy, to make the moment last. *Man, I thought they'd never take you out! Whooee! If Mrs. Fairburn could see me now!*

The Morganthals were waiting for him in front. Ignatz made a move to open the door for Mrs. Morganthal, but Maximilian Morganthal had a way with him. A slight toss of the head meant he would take it from there. As a courtesy to Ignatz, he touched his cap.

Kinda like I'm a real somebody. That's class, thought Ignatz. He scurried out a short distance from the house. From there he watched the car get smaller, until it disappeared through the gate.

He practiced tipping his cap like Max. *If I get rich, I'm gonna be nice as him and just as smooth. Mrs. Fairburn, she'd look like a queen, in a car like that.*

Maybe someday they'll let me drive her past my school. I'll 'specially not be late for graduation. When they hand me my high school diplomat, I'll roll it open, take the microphone, and kinda bow like I been practicing.

Then Mrs. Fairburn, she'll smile back at me. I'll stand tall like a Morganthal and say, Hear ye, hear ye! and make a exclamation of how I done it all for her.

Ignatz straightened his shoulders. *Man! A day to remember, that's for sure!*

Can It Last?

The chrome of the Duesenberg gleamed in the sun. "Perfect!" said Max, stroking the dashboard with his hand. The leather seats were soft as butter.

"Beautiful wife. Beautiful car. Beautiful day," he said. One meaningful glance at Mimi, and they both broke out in song—the same song.

Often their thoughts and words were shared and completed in this way. Each felt deep satisfaction in their oneness, with no need to express it.

In the past, they had danced together with a rare rhythm and style, drawing whispers of admiration. Above all, they did it to invoke envy.

Now, instead of wanting to be seen, they preferred to be alone. When he whispered in her ear, it was so she would press her cheek closer. Their joy on the dance floor came from blending together. Every move came from a refined intimacy of their souls.

In the earlier years of their marriage, he lavished her with jewels and furs for the world to see. But that had provided only a counterfeit happiness. Now he pampered her in a different way. His generosity was driven by an insatiable thirst

CHAPTER EIGHT

for her warm gaze, and she graciously invited his attention with a full heart.

"Can anything this good last forever?" said Mimi.

It gave him pleasure to see her so happy. "I love to look at you," he said.

Mimi thanked him with a touch. Her graceful hand lingered on his arm. He was overcome by a tingling sensation and flushed at the feel of it.

Out on the open road, the fresh sea breeze carried the perfume of wild blossoms. Mimi tried to identify the blue flowers in the field before them. She held her hair back from her eyes with both hands. Max pulled to the side so she could admire the view.

"Is it lupine?" she said. "I don't remember seeing it before." Though Max could be terse and blunt at times, Mimi knew his heart. She breathed deeply. "Maybe the world just comes alive when I'm with you."

A poem by William Cartwright had been on her mind.

He watched and listened as she recited the words.

There are two births: the one when light
First strikes the new awakened sense;
The other when two souls unite,
And we must count our life from thence,
When you loved me and I loved you,
Then both of us were born anew.

Love then to us new souls did give
And in those souls did plant new powers.
Since when another life we live,
The breath we breathe is his, not ours.
Love makes those young whom age doth chill,
And whom he finds young keeps young still.

For years, the cool elegance of her porcelain profile had seemed impenetrable. Now he marveled at what love had done to soften her features.

When they resumed driving, Mimi sighed. "Will you invite me to do this with you again?"

He had to force his eyes to watch the road. "Of course." He said. "You know how it is. I've got this obsession with beauty."

Each car passed slowly to allow the passengers to gawk at a real Duesenberg. They would never see another automobile like it on the road.

The sun was getting lower, and Max had to squint. It looked like something was running across the road. He swerved slightly. Was it a raccoon?

They would never know for sure. As the animal changed directions and ran toward them, Max slammed on the brakes.

Then Mimi screamed.

Maybe the front tire sank in a soft shoulder. No one would ever discover what happened. Or why it flipped over and over.

Entangled in fear, a sickening crunch propelled them through time and space. Blood and blackness separated them—then a ghastly nothingness.

A scream came from some unknown place deep inside him. "Mimi!"

But there was no answer.

Max crawled and stumbled up the incline like a madman. The mangled car lay upside down, fifteen yards above the bank where he had landed.

First he saw blood, then a pale hand.

A single wheel turned with an eerie squeak. The cream-colored frame hung over a rock. Mimi lay with her face crushed between them. Blood dripped and spattered across the unfeeling rock.

Max directed his cries to the road. "Help me! Someone help me!" But the last car must have moved on.

CHAPTER EIGHT

"I'm here, Mimi. It's all right," he said. "Please, be alive."

Sudden fear turned his face an ashen gray—the gas might explode.

Two young men saw the wreck and scrambled over the slope.

"My wife," cried Max, "Hurry!"

"Is she alive?"

"You idiots! Of course she's alive."

They worked to free her, but the taller boy asked. "Won't it crush her face, if we pull any harder?"

"Pull!"

Startled by his rage, the boys struggled and yanked.

The three of them carried her a safe distance from danger. Max gave them a grateful glance and cradled her limp body in his arms. He smelled her blood as it seeped through his fingers. She was motionless. Her cheeks had caved in, and her nose was ripped upward like a tent flap.

The shorter boy climbed to the road and flagged down a car.

A motley assortment of people gathered quickly, until a police car and ambulance appeared from nowhere and dispersed the crowd.

Max rocked Mimi gently, his teeth chattering. Did he see a subtle change in her color? Maybe in her heartbeat?

He watched in amazement as her mouth formed a silent scream, and she gasped.

"See . . . what did I tell you?" he whispered. Her blood felt sticky on his fingers.

He refused to be separated from Mimi as he climbed into the ambulance. But he couldn't look at her face.

CHAPTER NINE

Tell Him

Katrinka knew her embrace had startled Morgan, but if Hetty was upset enough to faint, it was definitely worthwhile. It gave Katrinka a perverse satisfaction to see Hetty on the ground beneath her.

She chortled triumphantly. "Why did you faint, Hetty dear? You look like you've seen a ghost!"

Hetty was pale, but did not otherwise appear distressed. "I must have stood up too fast," she said.

Katrinka realized her efforts had not produced the desired effect, and she tried to hide her disappointment. "Oh!" She said, "I'm sorry you're so frail, you poor dear! Let me help you up."

They sat together on the hammock.

When talking with Morgan earlier, Katrinka promised she would apologize to Hetty about her lies. She had intended to make a full confession. But Morgan was out of sight now. He wouldn't be able to hear their conversation, so she changed her mind.

Besides, why should she bother with the truth when there were more important considerations? She had to think of her future.

After a brief wait, Hetty said, "You have something to tell me?"

"Yes," said Katrinka. "It's just a funny little thing, really." But she didn't laugh or start an explanation. She cocked her head wistfully, looked down at her perfectly manicured hands, and sighed.

Her attention was on the rings Joseph had given her. The engagement ring wasn't dazzling like the one Morgan had given her years ago.

It's odd, she thought, *Hetty has such a pitiful gold band. Morgan could afford to buy her the Hope Diamond.*

She wondered if Morgan might soon surprise Hetty with a more impressive ring. Tilly reported seeing him in the jewelry store.

After a long pause, Hetty spoke. "What is it? Or would you rather have it come from Morgan? It sounds like something he knows about too."

"Oh, no! He doesn't. He just knew I had to talk to you." Her mind was no longer occupied by the immense diamond she once had. Tears gathered in her eyes. She didn't care that one of her Fanatalash false eyelashes was flopping loose.

She sighed. "It's something else. Oh, Hetty . . . I don't know what to do!" Panic contorted her features.

"We'll talk about it," said Hetty. "It's about the animal testing, isn't it?"

"No." Closing her eyes, Katrinka hoped Hetty could provide her with courage. She sucked in a gasping breath and said it.

"I'm not pregnant."

"What?" Hetty was stunned. She stared in disbelief.

"I never was," said Katrinka.

Hetty clenched her teeth and made no move to respond.

Katrinka gripped her hand. "I didn't lie to Joseph," she said, "but he came home just like Madame Vadoma said he would. Honest, I didn't lie. I just wrote and asked for his opinion about baby names."

She had finished her disclosure and now sobbed in great gulps. "What are we going to do? You can't tell anybody!" Her shoulders shook convulsively.

Hetty was slow to respond. "What does Joseph have to say about all this?"

The question startled Katrinka. She was embarrassed to answer, but she said, "He doesn't know."

"Then you can start with him."

"But he'll leave me!" wailed Katrinka. "He only came back because he thought there'd be a baby."

Hetty's expression was unmoved. She said, "If you love him, tell him."

This advice was completely unrealistic! But Katrinka had nowhere else to turn, now that her father was gone. It was comforting to have Hetty's arm around her, so it seemed best to nod in agreement.

Katrinka had an alternate plan. She could keep eating chocolates. If she gained enough weight, Joseph would continue to assume she was pregnant. At least it would give her time to think of something.

Sweet Comfort

Max paced anxiously in the emergency waiting room. The front of his jacket was smeared with blood, and his red-rimmed eyes told of exhaustion. In the corner, an old man looked up from reading *Life* magazine and quickly averted his eyes.

A young couple took turns at the payphone, talking in hushed tones. When they sat down, Max took their place, put a dime in the slot, and dialed Morgan.

"Get over here," he said. "No, the hospital."

Soon Morgan arrived. Max lurched toward him like a crazed animal. "They won't let me see Mimi," he said. The knuckles of his clenched fist were white with fury. "They haven't told me anything about her."

With a roar of anger and frustration, he glowered at the hands that were responsible. "I'm disgusted with myself. A small animal crossed the road, and I swerved."

Max was pale and haggard, but he dismissed Morgan's suggestion to have a doctor examine him. He shook his head and muttered, "A small animal."

Words never came easily in conversations with his father, but Morgan hoped to reassure him. "Dad, it was an accident," he said.

When leaving the cottage earlier, Morgan saw Hetty with her arm around Katrinka. They were deep in conversation. It seemed best not to interrupt them at the time. Now he phoned Hetty, and she quickly joined them at the hospital.

Morgan sensed Max had a rather cool attitude toward Hetty. It began as a mere impression, but was confirmed when Morgan heard them speaking privately.

"I never expected you to betray my confidence," said Max. The comment appeared to puzzle Hetty.

Morgan didn't mean to overhear them, and he retreated quietly.

Max continued. "When Mimi recovers, Katrinka will run to her and tattle. After that, Mimi won't want anything to do with me. I'm ruined."

He shook his head and changed the subject. "I've been grateful for our relationship the last few years. Nothing can erase those memories. The way we felt about each other—at least you gave us that."

Hetty opened her mouth, but before she could respond, the echo of footsteps in the hall stole her attention. A starched uniform rustled toward Max in the figure of a large nurse wearing a crisp white apron.

"Your wife will need to rest a while," she said. "This was only the first of the surgeries she'll need. The surgeon will

CHAPTER NINE

speak with you shortly, and I believe your family physician, Dr. Davidson, happens to be here on duty."

Producing a gown for Max, she assisted him with steady competence, as if it were an everyday occurrence to conceal the blood and dirt on hospital visitors.

About the same time, Katrinka arrived. She would have joined the Morganthals, but a flurry in the opposite direction caught her eye. Two men in hospital attire were wheeling a woman up from surgery. *Could it be Mimi?* Katrinka followed them down the hall to a spacious private room.

No one seemed to see her slip into a dark corner. They were all occupied with their patient. Then a sympathetic voice said, "Is this your mother?"

"Oh!" said Katrinka, "I didn't want her to be alone when she wakes up." The tears on her cheeks offered proof of her close relationship. When the last nurse left the room, Katrinka lowered her head with sincere sympathy.

Careful not to disturb Mimi, Katrinka held her hand gently. "How could this happen to you, of all people?" she said. Her tears flowed freely. "Oh, Mimi . . . I just know you're going to be all right," she whispered.

"Max will do everything in his power to make sure of it. You've been such a beautiful person, considering your age. And you will be again. We all love you so much! And Max would do anything for you, he's so proud of your looks. He should have taken better care of you. I think you have every right to be furious with him! Sometimes it helps to get angry, you know."

Bandages covered Mimi's face and one ear, but a narrow slit opened in one of her swollen eyes as if to encourage that line of thinking. Katrinka was happy to oblige.

She said, "It kind of helps us toughen up, when we get good and mad, don't you agree?" Then she whispered. "You don't need to answer. I think you're supposed to rest."

Katrinka tilted her head sweetly and squeezed Mimi's hand. "Maybe you should know . . . this isn't the *first* mistake

Max ever made. He may have ruined your face *temporarily*," she said, "but he ruined my Daddy's future *permanently*."

She thought their common bond of anger might comfort Mimi at such a painful time, so she continued. "I was going through a box of Daddy's old papers, and I learned a whole lot. There was this *New York Times* article. It talked about how circuses in America were disappearing.

"It said *Phil Wallace* was probably the one genius that could save the industry. The biggest circus in the world wanted Daddy! They offered him a *huge* executive position," she said. "He would have been set for life, if he'd gotten that job. But Max couldn't stand to lose him as a partner, so he lied about Daddy's character—just to be sure they wouldn't hire him! I saw a copy of the letter.

"Of course I don't hold it against Max," she said. "And if they can fix your face to where it looks good again, I'm sure *you'll* forgive him too."

She sat back in her chair.

A nurse bustled in to give Mimi a shot. "There now," she said. "You'll have a nice rest."

The door closed again, and Katrinka leaned in closer. Soon Mimi fell into a deep sleep. Weeping softly, Katrinka stroked her hand. "We'll get you through this, Mimi honey. Whatever damage Max has done, you'll always have me!" She blotted her tears and kissed Mimi's hand.

Minutes later Katrinka checked her appearance in the mirror of Mimi's private bathroom then joined the Morganthals in the waiting room. Without hesitation, she faced Max to offer special comfort. "Any time you need to rest," she said, "I'll stay by her side."

He answered nervously. "No. Please . . . no. Thanks, anyway."

Suddenly, a new idea became visible on Katrinka's face. "Max honey," she said, "I'm afraid there's something you need to know. I stopped at the gatehouse on my way here. You and

Mimi are so very, very vulnerable. I mean because of you both being here at the hospital, you know, for the foreseeable future."

Her large moist eyes searched his face, perhaps hoping to see gratitude for her imminent disclosure.

"I saw Ignatz . . . Oh, but I really hesitate to say anything!"

"Say it," said Max.

"Ignatz can't be trusted," she said. "I can't see how you can *possibly* have him at your place any longer. I've tried *so* hard to give him the benefit of the doubt! But Max, honey, I'm afraid he'll walk off with all your valuables."

Wistfully tilting her head, she raised her eyes to meet his with a sweet, convincing innocence. "I just now saw him with Freydis Fairburn's watch," she said. "It was her most treasured possession."

Morgan didn't wait for his father to answer. "If Ignatz has the watch," he said, "it means Freydis gave it to him."

"How can you be so sure, Morgan sweetheart? We need to be so cautious. Think of how he deceived us all so cruelly. Even to the point of changing his name." Katrinka rolled her eyes. "Really! Who is he, anyway, Beverley or Ignatz?"

She smiled, and the dimples in her soft pink cheeks captivated the strangers in the waiting room.

"I'm only thinking about you, Max honey. If Mimi's going to be disfigured," she said, "you shouldn't have *anything else* to worry about. You know how special you are to me."

Tilly on the Air

Another Saturday rolled around. Hetty sat at the microphone and watched the door. The radio studio audience was in place, but Tilly Teller was not. *If she doesn't come,* thought Hetty, *I'll have to interview people in the audience—or a staff member. That would be all right, but disappointing.*

Seconds before the deadline, Tilly appeared. Her entrance coincided perfectly with Hetty's introduction. Maybe no one else realized Tilly's cleverness, but Hetty was impressed with the seamless opening she had fashioned. The applause signs were unnecessary.

"So," said Tilly, "how does it feel to have a gossip columnist sitting across from you?" She laughed. It was a resonant stage laugh, and Hetty smiled back in admiration.

"Especially when I know so much about you and your family!" added Tilly. There was a wicked glint in her eye.

Hetty raised the microphone and said, "I think I feel about the way you feel. You see, my business is much like yours. It's all about gossip, and I'm eager to let people find out more about you."

Tilly laughed her fabulously theatrical laugh again. "Nothing could be as juicy as talking about the Morganthals," she said, "and people like them. That's what keeps me in business."

Suddenly, she altered her inflection to sound more subdued. "First," she said, "I was sorry to hear about your mother-in-law. What a tragedy. It just proves you can't mix drinking and driving."

"Thank you, Tilly. I'll pass along your sympathy. In this case, Maximilian Morganthal proved what we already knew—that accidents sometimes happen to careful drivers. But tell me a little about you—something our listeners don't know."

Tilly was prepared. "Our listeners will know me best, if they hear me at work," she said, "so I propose to interview *you*." She leaned toward the microphone and opened the notebook she always carried.

"Very well," said Hetty, "but to make sure we're *both* glad you came," she said, "we'll have to compromise. I'll begin. You see, you don't have a monopoly on gossip. I know a little about *your* family too."

She smiled, but left no opening for Tilly to speak. "Let's talk about your father, Halston Teller," she said. "Here's what I

You see, you don't have a monopoly on gossip.

learned—" Hetty thought of Katrinka's advice. She had said, *Make her squirm*. She had also told of Halston Teller's brush with the law.

Tilly Teller stiffened, and her face lost its color.

Hetty kept talking. "About your father—tell us what he did when you were in the ninth grade. I know he was a writer, too."

"Ninth grade?" said Tilly.

"Yes," said Hetty. "I followed a rumor. I hope to get it right. I'm told you wrote a short play, with your father's encouragement. Tell us about it—and what your father did."

Tilly straightened. Relief appeared to wash the dread from her face. "The school put on my play," she said. "It was a silly little thing, really."

Her words tumbled out as if she were still a ninth grader again. "After that, my father mentored a lot of aspiring young writers. He made it fun—and very competitive. It spread to become a regional contest. He was the inspiration. But for various reasons, Dad never got the credit."

"You must have been very fond of your father."

"Yes, I was," said Tilly. She looked down and fiddled with her notebook. "He was a misunderstood man. He's dead now, but the competition is still going strong—one act plays, journalism, essays, and so on. It's called *The Capital High School Literary Program.*"

"I believe you're mistaken." Hetty locked eyes with her guest.

"That's what it's called," said Tilly.

"Not anymore. As of three days ago, it's known as the *Halston Teller Literary Award.*"

"What?"

"Yes. When it was brought to their attention, the vote was unanimous." Hetty produced a letter. "This is to you from the board."

Tilly tore open the envelope, oblivious to the unseen listeners. "I hardly know what to say!" She struggled to

CHAPTER NINE

maintain control of her emotions. "He was not a perfect man . . . I'm so grateful."

"You can thank the school," said Hetty, "and the people who want to recognize your father for the contribution he made."

For the moment, Tilly appeared dazed. Hetty filled the silence with small talk until her guest could continue.

The awkwardness ended when Tilly smiled and said, "I believe it's my turn to ask *you* a thing or two."

She hesitated then closed her notebook—perhaps to reconsider her plan of attack.

The Hospital

Morgan worried about his mother. But perhaps even more about his father. Max frequently sent fresh flowers to Mimi's hospital room, but he was denied permission to visit.

No one was able to change Mimi's mind. Though nurses and doctors came and went, she showed little interest in anything. Her conversation was limited to the courtesies that came naturally.

Hetty tried to coordinate the visits of friends and family around the complicated hospital schedule. Dan and Dora Lawrence helped by caring for Pippa. Marian and Leaf were equally attentive. They all called on Mimi and hoped it was the right thing to do.

After the accident, Morgan had phoned his sister Melinda, who came immediately to be with her mother. He wondered if she would marry Dart Duncan and settle nearby. Dart had been in and out of her life for years.

Through much of their courtship, Dart appeared to have one eye on Katrinka Wallace. It had caused a rather rocky five-year engagement, but Katrinka was out of circulation now, so Morgan thought they might be making plans.

When Melinda was in the sixth grade, Morgan had encouraged her to cultivate a friendship with Hetty. With pleasure, he now watched the two of them on the other side of Mimi's bed.

Morgan looked at Hetty. She sat tall, speaking softly to Melinda. The light seemed to gather around her, weaving and floating through the pale puffs of her hair.

A miracle had happened in this very hospital. Was Hetty thinking of it too? Memories carried Morgan through time and space.

Even now reality seemed to verge on a dream. He had been near death. Dauntless determination had driven Hetty to his bedside. Afraid of being too late, she could not be restrained. She had pressed her head against his chest, straining to hear his heartbeat until she was sure he was alive. Her tears of relief ended all pretense of distance between them. Every breath they shared renewed his strength, and together they flew above the clouds to a place of love and light. Even now the dream was vivid.

Hetty looked up at him. When their eyes met, she smiled, and her cheeks colored. Yes, she knew his thoughts. They shared the memory.

Morgan's focus changed abruptly when the surgeon entered with two young nurses. They had come to remove Mimi's bandages. Morgan stood. There was only small talk as they all waited. Suspense made every remark seem insignificant. Someone wondered why all hospital rooms were painted green. Occasional meaningless laughter only heightened the anxiety.

When the bandages were off, the shock of Mimi's appearance seemed to suck air from the room.

Following a long pause, Hetty spoke to Mimi. "I know you didn't want Max here, but he's well represented by the beautiful flowers he's sent."

CHAPTER NINE

"They say the discoloration should be gone soon," said Melinda. "Isn't that right?" No one seemed to hear her question. Maybe they were just pretending not to hear.

The largest of Mimi's wounds required attention for a time. When a young nurse discarded the last of the bandages, she spoke up in a cheery voice. "It is what it is," she said, "but aren't you amazed what modern medicine can accomplish?"

"Yes! Oh, yes!" said Melinda. Her wild enthusiasm veiled an unspoken rebuttal. She stepped from the room briefly to compose herself.

Morgan took his mother's hand in both of his. "Dad's always here, you know." Mimi looked at him with a face he hardly recognized.

She faced the ceiling with a blank stare. "I'll want a mirror sometime," she sighed. "For now, I'd like to sleep."

"Time should make this easier," he said.

Hearing a familiar voice in the hall, Morgan stepped out to see Dr. Davidson. He might have some information about his mother's condition.

"Hey, there!" said the doctor. With every smile, his nose spread across his face. He reached out to pump Morgan's hand.

"We've been indebted to you over the years," said Morgan. "Can you tell me what to expect?"

The doctor was more serious now.

"Well, I'm sure you know to take good care of her. Don't take any more chances with her life. One close call is enough."

"Accidents happen," said Morgan.

"They do," said the doctor, "but in her case, let's have no more accidents."

Another smile, and his nose broadened again. "I'm sure your little girl will keep up her spirits."

Morgan thought of the pictures Pippa had drawn for her grandmother Mimi. He and Hetty felt honor-bound to explain, in detail, what each one depicted.

The doctor continued. "My cousin has eleven children. I can't help suspecting one or two were accidents," he said, "but that was all right. *She* didn't have a heart condition like your wife."

Morgan chuckled. "Oh, you were talking about Hetty! I agree we can't take any chances. But actually, it's my mother's condition I was asking about."

"Oh, of course . . . your mother! Sorry I misunderstood." He laughed. "She'll be fine. She and Max are both lucky to be alive."

The doctor departed, and before Morgan could glance around for Max, he felt his hand on his shoulder.

"Tell me about Mimi," said his father.

"Well, they took off the bandages . . ."

"I know," said Max, "she's going to recover." He waved his hand. "And what else?"

He indicated a couch, and they sat together. Morgan didn't know anything for sure, so his best answer was nothing at all. They both stared at the clock on the wall. It was broken.

"Mimi and I—we had plans," said Max. He tapped his fist on the arm of the couch. "Now it's too late." The reflection from the walls gave a greenish cast to his face.

He sighed. "Maybe I'll go with you to Cape Town when you meet with Chipperfield's Circus people. We'll get some fresh ideas for an act. There's not much left for me now, except performing."

"We should talk another time," said Morgan.

"No," said Max. "What have you decided? Tell me now."

Experience told Morgan he couldn't put off the answer. "Well, I knew you were waiting," he said. "So I went down to the river to think. I wanted to be alone, but Katrinka followed me there.

"Funny how the mind works. While we were talking I saw my life laid out ahead of me as a series of choices. It suddenly became clear to me. That's when I knew what to do."

Morgan looked directly at Max. "This decision . . . it's hard to tell you, Dad." He looked down and cracked his knuckles. "I'm sorry. I won't be working out a contract for our partnership. I want more time with Hetty."

Seldom had Morgan opposed his father. Now he waited for the trouble that would surely follow. But Max hardened the line of his jaw, and that seemed to be the end of it.

Had all anger between them been spent years ago? Morgan hoped so.

Perhaps his father deserved a more complete explanation, so Morgan continued. "Hetty's been struggling with what's most important to her," he said. "Whatever she wants, I'm not going to hold her back. When she started her radio program, I tried to clip her wings. I was wrong to do that. Whatever she decides, I want to be with her—not against her."

There was no response. The green walls heard nothing but the ticking of the broken clock. Max stared up at the jerking minute hand and frowned.

Morgan leaned against the arm of the couch and looked down the hall to his mother's room. Hetty was in there.

Suddenly nothing else mattered. She was only a few yards away, but he ached with the separation. He realized how seldom he told her his feelings. He felt so much a part of her that words seemed unnecessary. So strong were his sentiments that he assumed she shared them. Did she sense it as much as he did?

In the intensity of his emotions, Morgan received a flash of understanding. He could see the utter tragedy of his father's situation. Max felt the sorrow of his wife's rejection. Now he suffered another blow; the dream of performing with his son was over.

Max stood slowly. Grief was in his stooped shoulders and red-rimmed eyes. He said, "That was the right decision, Son."

Morgan stood and clasped his father's hand. It was more than a handshake. It spoke of shared understanding and the likelihood of more to come.

Max was slow to release their clasp.

I Can Count

Katrinka stood at her kitchen counter. The last light of early evening slanted through the crisp white curtains. She had prepared a surprise for Joseph. But would he sense the butterflies in her stomach? A small secret smile turned up the corners of her glossy pink lips.

Maybe they could start by discussing Mimi's progress. Katrinka could see Max was home from the hospital, wandering through the gardens. That probably meant Mimi's bandages had been removed.

Joseph was in the living room reading. In her most captivating voice, Katrinka called to him. "You can come in now, Honeybun!"

She surprised him with an elaborately decorated chocolate cake from a first class bakery. To add a homey touch, she wore a pretty white apron. It had a pocket large enough to hold the oversized card she would soon give him.

"Happy Birthday, honey," she said. "I didn't light the candles. You know how wax always drips on the icing."

His birthday was still a week away, but Katrinka was far too excited to wait for the actual day. Though he didn't look at her face, Joseph thanked her pleasantly.

His mind seemed far away. That was all right. He would be happy enough, in a minute.

Katrinka's fingers closed around the card. It had been awkward to write about such a delicate matter. She thought of the message.

> *My Darling Joseph,*
>
> *I've got some exciting news! We now have a definite date for when the baby is due. It has changed from two months to six months away, instead. You can circle February 13th on the calendar. I checked, and it's NOT a Friday.*
>
> *I would NEVER want any secrets between*

CHAPTER NINE

us. When you came back from Africa you had the impression I was pregnant, but I know you will forgive yourself (and me) for being wrong.

It was all a misunderstanding, and I hope you will remember I never lied to you.

My love for you has got so huge I can't hardly believe my own eyes! That's why I didn't dare take the chance of telling you before.

I'm so very, very proud to be your wife, and our baby will be proud to have you be his (or her) daddy, too!

Your loving and devoted wife,
Katrinka

The doctor had called her with the news. This time it was true. Katrinka spent time in the closet where the shower gifts were hidden. The baby powder, the stack of diapers, the flannel blankets—suddenly everything seemed wonderful in a new and different way. She reopened the box containing the soft yellow sweater and felt the little duck embroidered on it. It was soft against her cheek.

Joseph would be happy, too. Certainly he would forgive her! But she would have to prepare him first. Standing behind his chair, Katrinka put her cheek against his.

"Guess what, sweetheart!" she said. She waited. When he didn't play her guessing game, she said, "I've decided to take your name! From now on, I want everybody to call me Katrinka Ostler." She kissed his cheek.

Joseph took his time to cut the cake. Carefully, he placed a piece on each of the two plates in front of him and turned the plates so the forks were at precisely three o'clock. Katrinka straightened up and held her breath. Wasn't he going to say anything?

Where his fork touched the fudge icing, he smeared it a moment or two before he spoke. "Interesting initials," he said. "K.O. It makes perfect sense. You're a Knock Out. Always have been."

Was that all he would say? Katrinka hugged him from behind. He seemed to be thinking of something else.

She felt her throat tighten. "What's the matter, Joseph?"

"Please sit down," he said. "You may want to reconsider the name. Though I do appreciate it." He put down his fork.

Katrinka circled the table and sat across from him. "No! No, I want your name. I really want to be your wife in every way. Please say you want me to!"

Something was terribly wrong. Where was the jovial face she knew? Joseph's somber expression was strange. It frightened her, but she loved him all the more.

He didn't tilt back in his chair with his thumbs in his belt. He didn't toss back his head and laugh, or call her Trink. He touched her hand and spoke slowly. "I know there's no baby." He said. "I suspected it soon after I got home."

Katrinka saw pity and disappointment in his eyes, and it confused her.

He continued. "I'm no dunce," he said. "I can count backwards from nine, and you're not filling out in the right places."

Katrinka's hands trembled, and her head felt wobbly. She stood quickly, tipping over the chair, and ran to face the window. Joseph mustn't see her tears. It was so complicated.

"About you and me," he said, "it's not going to work. I'll be going back to Africa. I've stopped waiting for your honesty, but I was hoping to see some kindness."

Katrinka felt numb. His sickening words echoed in her head. This couldn't be real.

Joseph wasn't through. "Your comments about Hetty, at the press conference," he said, "that was the last nail in the coffin. Every disaster seems to have your fingerprints on it."

She closed her eyes and groped for the faucet. It was cold and hard. And real like Joseph's words. Her fingers wanted to

CHAPTER NINE

reach in her pocket for the card—to let him know the baby was real this time. But now it was too late.

Katrinka took a shuddering breath and looked outside. A shadowy figure on the lawn belonged to Max. He looked dejected. Somehow his sadness seemed vaguely connected with hers. Maybe it was.

Joseph stood. "Whatever you decide about the name," he said, "it doesn't matter to me one way or the other."

Katrinka clapped her hands over her ears. They had come to a fork in the road, and she had to think.

I can't look at him. He mustn't see how much I love him.

He only came home to me because he thought he was going to be a father. Nothing more. He doesn't love me enough. If I never see Joseph again, at least I'll have his baby. But I won't tell him.

Will the baby be a dwarf like Daddy? He might grow up tall like Joseph. I was hoping we could find out together. Maybe I can be the kind of mother that would make him proud. Meanwhile, how do I hold my life together?

Max might be the key! I'll find a way, but I've got to get rid of Ignatz so he won't talk.

Everybody says it's just a matter of time before Morgan runs for Congress. When it happens, I might think up a few secrets about him. And when I start talking to the press, nobody will know if they're true or not. I wonder if I can still count on Tilly to help.

Either way, when I'm in front of the camera, I control my destiny. I have big plans for LuvCon, once I get Hetty out of my hair. One way or the other, my child is going to grow up like a Morganthal, but I need a plan.

The card stayed in her pocket.

Picketers

The demonstrators were loud and unruly. Katrinka felt like a prisoner in her own office. She checked the pink LuvCon clock on her desk. It was almost five o'clock. Fortunately, Hetty would come to her rescue in a few minutes.

Katrinka would have escaped long ago if they weren't picketing near her car in the parking lot. She looked at the crowd through a crack in the blinds, but her mind was on Joseph. Could he be at the airport yet? She thought of that morning and her conversation with him. It would be their last.

When he phoned, she was still asleep. Joseph had been staying at his sister's house and explained the reason for his call—as if he needed one. Marian would be inviting her to a family supper.

Hetty and her parents, Dan and Dora Lawrence, were also invited. Katrinka wanted to decline the invitation, but Joseph said, "Please go. Eat her food and be grateful she invited you."

Apparently Joseph's luggage was packed and waiting by the door. Morgan would soon pick him up on his way to the office. Between personal calls and errands, his entire day would be full until time for Morgan to take him to the airport.

When he heard a knock on the door, Joseph said a hasty goodbye.

Katrinka heard the phone click. It was over, and she hadn't said she loved him. Even her last goodbye had caught in her throat. She sat at the edge of the bed, unable to hang up the receiver. There was a dial tone, then more noise. The tears welled up and overflowed.

Still Katrinka gripped the phone. Heavy sobs shook her frame. Both hands pressed the telephone to her heart, and then trembling, moved it down. Down to seek a second tiny heartbeat.

The phone went silent. At last a deep and merciful sleep overtook her.

CHAPTER NINE

An hour later, her eyes opened to a fresh beginning. She had things to do, and she would do them. She closed her eyes in the shower and let it cleanse her face like gentle rain.

It would be all right to get to the office late. People would call. Fine. Her secretary knew how to cover for her. She would answer as she was directed. The most convincing phrase was I'm sorry, Miss Wallace has just stepped out.

It wasn't necessarily a lie. After all, there was always a chance Katrinka could, at any given moment, step out from wherever she happened to be—the shower, for instance.

From now on, her secretary must address her as Mrs. Ostler.

Katrinka rehearsed it aloud. "Mrs. Ostler has just stepped out," she said.

No, that would never do. How about the truth? She pursed her lips and imitated the nasal voice of her secretary. "I'm sorry, Mrs. Ostler hasn't come in yet. She's rather pregnant, you see, and felt like taking an extra long shower this morning. May I tell her who called?"

As she picked up her car keys, Katrinka glanced in the mirror and imagined Joseph's face behind her. It was an honest face with an open friendliness. Katrinka knew very well he wasn't there, but she winked at him anyway then laughed and played her dimples just for him.

According to the pink LuvCon clock, five o'clock had come and gone. Katrinka was exhausted after a long day at the office. Hetty was late. Where could she be? She was forever getting lost.

Katrinka started toward the window, but heard a noise in the hall.

"Hetty, is that you?" She opened her office door. Two men from security were just checking to see if she was all right. The tilt of her head and the display of her little pearly-white teeth rewarded them for their manly protection.

She sat back in her chair and tried not to think of Joseph. Everything reminded her of Joseph. Had she made a huge mistake? She couldn't stop wondering.

If I had told Joseph about the baby, he'd still be here.

Why is Marian having me come to this dinner? Is it because Joseph asked her to? Maybe he pities me. I'll never know whether I still matter to him.

I'm glad Hetty offered to pick me up. How else could I get out of here? I told her to come through the underground loading dock. She'll see why soon enough.

She couldn't possibly deal with the crowd out front. She lacks the skill. They'd want her head on a pike!

Katrinka realized she had been caught up in her own thoughts for a very long time. Nothing much seemed to be going on outside. How long ago did the ugly commotion die down? Maybe the picketers had left. She walked to the window again and peered cautiously through the blinds.

Many of the demonstrators had put down their signs and sat facing the entrance. Several news trucks were parked near the crowd. *Where did they all come from? Who called them?* Among the reporters, Katrinka recognized several familiar faces. Why was Tilly Teller there?

The crowd was subdued. A harmonious ripple of laughter spread through the gathering. Who was outside the entrance speaking to them? Katrinka couldn't see straight down below her, so she eased in close to the window. Somebody held their attention.

It was Hetty Morganthal.

Make Him Go Away

Before Max left for the hospital, Marian called and invited him to a family supper. He declined politely enough, but

CHAPTER NINE

his response seemed laced with mild hostility. Maybe it had taken courage for Marian to ask him on such short notice. He doubted whether she would try again.

Now Max posted himself outside Mimi's hospital room as usual. There was little point to it, but he did it anyway. The nurses were accustomed to the dark-haired, brooding gentleman. As Hetty approached, he stood with a cool, impersonal courtesy that puzzled her.

The medicinal smell of the sickroom offended Hetty's nose, and she opened Mimi's window to let in the morning air. A sweet blend of moldering leaves and late-blooming flowers drifted in and gradually changed the mood. Hetty thought so, anyway.

Maybe Mimi did too, because she said, "It's good of you, Hetty." That was all she said for a time, but her eyes followed Hetty around the room.

Every morning, some of the flowers needed fresh water. Others were ready to be discarded to make room for more. Most of them had a card indicating Max had sent them. Hetty straightened the sheets. "He's still here, Mimi," she said. "He's always here, hoping to see you."

Mimi hesitated. Could she be waiting to hear more about Max? Apparently she was not, because she spoke again. "I know he is. But he can't come in. You understand why." She was waiting for Hetty to agree, but she didn't.

Mimi looked out the window. "You do see, don't you? I want him to go away . . . so he'll remember when we were happy together." She seemed perfectly composed.

Hetty squeezed her hand, but said nothing.

Mimi was forced to continue. "I want him to be free of me now," she said.

The scars had left Mimi's features with such a different cast that it was difficult to read her thoughts. Hetty waited in vain for Mimi to retract those words, but instead, she added more.

"I wish this were easier," said Mimi. "Tell Max to go away. Please find a way to explain it's over. You do understand my feelings, don't you, Hetty?"

"Yes. I understand perfectly."

Hetty promised she would confront him as soon as possible.

CHAPTER TEN

Kindness

Katrinka waited for Hetty at the gatehouse. In a few minutes, they would go to LuvCon together. Hetty had invited the picketers to come back in a few days and tour the animal testing labs. The two of them had considerable planning to do before that time.

When she looked out the door and saw Hetty's hair, Katrinka insisted she should come inside. "What happened to you, honey?"

It wasn't as if Hetty looked any worse than usual. But she was going out in public, so something *must* be done.

"I just washed it," said Hetty. "Isn't it dry yet?"

"It's just that . . . well, the way it got burned in back . . . you look like a cocker spaniel."

"Is that bad?"

Hetty was obviously a hopeless case, but Katrinka resisted rolling her eyes and changed the subject, instead.

"Tilly says she saw Morgan in the jewelry store. You can be sure he's getting you a gorgeous diamond!"

"What would I do with a diamond?" said Hetty. "He gave me the band I wanted."

How exasperating! Hetty was so dense.

"Hetty honey, he's a man! What do you expect? Don't you know anything? He wants to give you things!"

Katrinka realized she would have to be absolutely desperate before asking Hetty's advice about anything. *I'm not desperate,* she thought, *or am I?*

She poked and pulled at Hetty's hair then gathered it in back with a pink ribbon. "Aren't you going to look in the mirror?"

After a quick glance, Hetty laughed and said, "Maybe you should go into the beauty business."

This was actually fun. It would probably be easy to talk with Hetty about Joseph—and about the baby. All in good time.

Katrinka couldn't forget her private talk with Morgan. He had refused to give her any marital advice. It was so exasperating! She thought surely *someone* must know how to keep a husband happy. Morgan had said, *That would be Hetty.*

Even though it was over between her and Joseph, Katrinka thought it wouldn't hurt to get some advice. Morgan would be in New York for ten days. During his absence, she and Hetty would be together more than usual. For one thing, there was tomorrow night's supper at Leaf and Marian's.

As they left the gatehouse and walked toward Hetty's car, Katrinka saw Ignatz. She couldn't get in the car fast enough to avoid him.

He ran up, quite out of breath, and doffed his cap. "I'm real heartbroke for you, ma'am," he said. "And I been thinking. You know Shakespeare? He wrote this play, see. It's called *Taming of the Shrew*. It's got this real intrinsic plot. Man, you can't hardly tell who's who! Anyways, there's this doll in it. She ain't worth two cents, excepting she's a real looker. No offense, but she made me think of you.

"Your Mr. Ostler, he was one fantastic guy. And you can bet he's gonna tame his shrew! It's gonna be okay!"

He opened the door for Katrinka. "You and him—I hope you get a real happy ending," he said.

He seemed to mean it. Katrinka was speechless with surprise.

The Dear Ruins

Max stood at the door of Mimi's hospital room again the next morning. He was waiting for the fresh flowers he had ordered to be delivered. At last an arrangement of yellow roses and baby's breath swept past him and into her room.

He would force himself to leave now and never again come to the hospital. He had made a fool of himself.

Just when he was struggling to go, Hetty came from behind. He knew her footsteps and turned to face her. "Hetty, about yesterday morning—I was rude."

There was no dignity to his expression—only a profound sadness, and he lacked the energy to stand erect. "I know Mimi wants you to send me away, but you don't have to," he said. "I'm going.

"Oh no, Max. You misunderstood," she said. Hetty smiled as if everything was just fine. "Can we talk a minute?" she asked.

This would undoubtedly be about his treatment of Phil; maybe at last Hetty was going to apologize for betraying his confidence. They went to the couch. Max didn't have the energy to be angry. He was beyond caring.

Hetty took his hand. There was a vague memory of how he had felt as a child. He thought of Phil Wallace, his childhood friend.

Now Hetty pulled a book from her purse and opened it. She read to him and talked of Thomas Moore. Max was familiar with the poem he wrote. And the song. Moore's wife was scarred by smallpox, and he had sung it to her.

"How can Mimi resist your voice?" said Hetty. "You can't give up, when she loves you so much."

"I don't believe you. I heard what she said."

"Well, she she feels ugly. Mimi doesn't want you to see her that way."

"You think I care how she looks? There's nobody like Mimi."

"But she's afraid you'll reject her."

His eyes smoldered. "Don't tell me a fairy tale." He became silent and tapped his fist on the arm of the couch. Then he remembered something Phil had said. *Don't look where you don't want to go*.

Max did not want to go into a future without Mimi.

He stared at Hetty. Her hands were trembling, but she gave him the book and said, "You have nothing to lose."

Some of the color returned to his face as he read the words. Max knew the poem, and so did Mimi, but he would read from the book anyway. He stood at Mimi's door with little confidence. "I'll sing the second verse," he said.

Hetty nodded, and Max wondered why she looked so ill at ease.

He began singing.

> *"It is not while beauty and youth are thine own,*
> *And thy cheeks unprofan'd by a tear,*
>
> *That the fervour and faith of a soul can be known,*
> *To which time will but make thee more dear!"*

It had started badly. Max should have warmed up his voice. How stupid to sing in a hospital hall! The nurses probably thought he was crazy—emotionally unbalanced.

His voice cracked, but he kept singing anyway.

> *"Oh! the heart, that has truly lov'd, never forgets,*
> *But as truly loves on to the close;*

CHAPTER TEN

As the sun-flower turns on her god, when he sets,
The same look which she turn'd when he rose!"

Not a sound was heard from Mimi's room, and Max couldn't hide his disappointment. Hetty had made up the whole scheme. He was sure of it. He should be furious, but he felt nothing.

When Hetty stood up, he wondered what crazy idea she had in mind now.

"I wonder if Mimi could be asleep," she said. Hetty still looked uneasy, but she took the door handle.

Then they both heard a small, thin, magically wonderful sound.

"Max . . ."

He ran to her quickly. She had been weeping. Her face turned slowly toward her husband, and they embraced. Max knelt and his eyes explored every part of her face, hungry to memorize her scars. They would be a new and dear way to prove his love was unchanged.

"I want you home," he said. He tightened his arms around her again. "I want you . . . "

"But I have more surgeries."

She felt the furrow in his forehead. "Too many days without you, Max."

He was troubled, and Mimi could see pain in his expression. "What is it?" she asked.

He had to tell her. There was no other way.

"Maybe you know. I should have told you about this, years ago," he said. "I'm not worthy of you. There's something I've done. Something awful.

"I didn't want you to hear it from someone else. But maybe you have. It's about Phil."

Mimi put her hand over his mouth. "Yes, I know," she said. "I already know. I won't hear any more about it. You've spent your life being fair to Phil. You're an honorable man."

She pulled his head to rest against her chest.

"It's been a nightmare," he said. "I was sure you'd be through with me if you found out. I thought I'd go mad . . . tried drinking . . . but it didn't help."

He shook his head. "I can't believe Hetty would pass along something like that, after I confided in her."

"Hetty?" Mimi was confused. "She didn't. It was Katrinka. She found some letters in a box."

Max scowled. "Not Hetty? What's the matter with me! I've been a hothead. An idiot." He would go to Hetty later and make amends.

For the moment, he wanted only to hold Mimi.

There was life, and love, and a future, all rising from the dear ruins.

The Supper

Max held a bouquet of dahlias and knocked at Leaf and Marian's front door. Though he had declined the invitation, Hetty insisted they would still want him at dinner. Maybe they just needed him to fill in for Morgan, who was on a business trip.

Leaf greeted him warmly. But where was the hostess? How could he give the flowers to Marian, if he couldn't locate her?

Oh, there she was—in the kitchen. She wiped the spaghetti sauce from her fingers onto a tea towel and extended her hand. Her smile was bright, and her freckles stood out on her pink face. She was sorry not to have met him at the door. It was the broken doorbell—she meant to get it fixed years ago.

Hetty's mother, Dora Lawrence, was at the stove. Her friendly manner put Max at ease right away. She put the flowers in a vase for Marian and asked if he would mind taking the salad bowl to the dining room.

When he did, he found Dan Lawrence trying to fit miscellaneous chairs around the table. "Oh, ho!" said Dan. "Here's the man." He had a hefty grip and an easy manner.

CHAPTER TEN

Max had been uncertain how to conduct himself at such an informal gathering, but it was no longer a concern. They really did seem to want him.

Occasionally Pippa and Danny peeked bashfully from around the corner. The children wore costumes they must have found in the basement.

Pippa ran to her grandpa Dan, crying about an injustice. It wasn't fair that Danny always got to be her uncle. Why couldn't she be the uncle some of the time? Dan dried her tears and established peace.

Max wondered at Dan's natural, easy way with children. He looked on with respect and thought of all the experiences he and Mimi could never recapture with their family. But for now he was fortunate to be an observer, and that would have to do. This was no time for regrets. They would make other memories.

Max had almost convinced himself of this when he felt Pippa's tiny hand in his. He touched her soft curls, and she looked up at him, eyes shining under her pale eyelashes. She smiled and was gone.

His granddaughter had come to him just because she wanted to.

Did someone knock? Leaf wasn't sure, but he opened the door to welcome Hetty and Katrinka. Pippa ran to Hetty and hugged her legs.

"Mommy, Mommy!" she squealed. Pandemonium ruled. Strangely, Max found the confusion pleasurable. He was content to stand alone with his thoughts, but his contemplation ended when Katrinka sidled up to him.

"Max, darling!" she said, "I never dreamed I'd see you here!" She lowered her voice tactfully. "This is not exactly our kind of place, is it, honey?"

Hearing no signs of agreement, she said, "How's our sweet Mimi?"

"Sleeping," he said.

Katrinka sighed. "Mimi was always such a beautiful hostess," she said, "but it's so tragic the way things change." She turned her face up to him and fanned her long eyelashes. "It's hard to be alone in the world, isn't it? But you'll always have me, Max honey. Any time you need me, I'm just a stone's throw away."

Her long pink fingernails poked into the palm of his hand when she squeezed it. "We're two of a kind, aren't we, Max?" She winked and tossed her hair.

Katrinka's overwhelming pinkness and the suffocating waves of her perfume revolted Max. "No," he said. He was relieved when Marian called Katrinka into the kitchen.

Hetty came to the dining room. Maybe now he could say something to her. While she put place cards around the table, she said the names to herself.

A blue ribbon had come loose, and her hair was poking out on one side.

Her back was to him. He cleared his throat, and she turned around.

"You made it all up," he said. "The whole fairy tale. You had no idea if Mimi would let me in."

"Well, I admit it," said Hetty.

Max didn't want to make her feel guilty. He was simply searching for a good way to thank her.

"Why did you do it?" he asked. He didn't mean to sound gruff.

Hetty gasped for air. "Well, because Mimi said things I didn't believe. Then she asked if I understood her feelings, and I did." Suddenly, Hetty appeared confident. "I understood her perfectly. It didn't matter what she said. I only cared about what she really meant."

Max tried to think of another way to thank her.

"Turn around," he said. "Let me tie your ribbon." Maybe this way he wouldn't have to face her and put his emotions on display.

CHAPTER TEN

Hetty's hair didn't look any better when he was through. But it had been an excuse to show his affection. With his hands touching her shoulders, he choked out his words of gratitude. They might serve as an apology, as well.

Hetty turned and hugged him as he hoped she would. In response, he tightened his grip and thanked her again.

Dinner began, and Pippa didn't want to sit in a high chair. She perched instead on two telephone books that wouldn't stay in place.

Max found his place card to Marian's right and helped seat her. As he pushed in her chair, the bright copper color of her hair took him by surprise. It was the perfect complement to her open and friendly intelligence.

He wondered—was there anything Marian and Katrinka might have in common? He had his doubts. Maybe that's why she had placed her sister-in-law at the far end of the table. Joseph was probably their only connection.

Katrinka sat to the right of Leaf, and Dan was on the other side of her. She seemed quite cheerful, flanked by Hetty's two fathers. They were showing her how to wind spaghetti on her fork.

Dora went to the kitchen for a stack of dishtowels and tied one around Katrinka's neck. Other kind gestures followed that one. Dora continued to mother her with every possible show of attention, until Katrinka appeared very much at ease.

Max thought of the time he and Phil sucked their spaghetti to make it flip sauce at the end. His mother was angry and didn't want him to play with Phil anymore. That had further solidified their friendship.

Max smiled and disappeared into his thoughts.

Maybe Katrinka just needs to know people care about her. If only Phil could see her now. It's amazing how Hetty has tolerated her all these years—and even sticks up for her.

When we put Katrinka in charge of LuvCon, it was really just for show. It seemed like a good idea at first. But Hetty didn't think it was fair to use her as just a pretty face.

Maybe with Hetty's help she'll become more than a figurehead. She's basically clever. I hope Phil's influence will show through at some point.

Marian thanked Dora Lawrence for bringing the delicious spinach salad. Hetty had made the cinnamon rolls, and her papa Dan had poured the water. Many hands had boiled the spaghetti and made the sauce. Leaf's apple pie was in the oven.

By process of elimination, Max figured that Marian must have cooked the peas. After accepting a second serving, he complimented her on their flavor. She laughed quite cheerfully and said, "They did turn out nice and round." Marian's friendly humility charmed him.

The children ate quietly, but Danny spoke up when the grownups left a break in the conversation. "Uncle Max," he asked, "when are you and Morgan going to be clowns?"

Max had a letter in his vest pocket and was waiting for an opportunity to tell about the contents. "Morgan just sent me this," he said. "It's from the International Circus Clowns Club. There's an unwritten law among clowns. You don't copy each other's makeup. To make sure of it, a man in England keeps a record of our makeup designs."

Max held a photograph so Danny could see it from across the table. "They're done on chicken eggs with the insides blown out," he said. "Morgan just registered Phil and me."

Danny's eyes were wide with wonder. "Wow!" he said.

Katrinka appeared every bit as excited as five-year-old Danny. Morgan had included a second photograph of Phil Wallace. He knew Katrinka would treasure anything concerning her father. Max passed it to her. "Keep it," he said. "Notice how Morgan had them made. Those are actual samples of our wigs."

How did Morgan think of things like that? He was like Mimi in some ways. They could both start a good conversation.

Max was sorry he and his son didn't have much in common. On the other hand, they shared a concern for living creatures.

He had been with Morgan once when a bird flew into a plate glass window. It fell lifeless on the sidewalk before them. Morgan had held the bird, cradling its soft and fragile form in his hands until it perched on his finger and flew away.

Even if they couldn't succeed with a sanctuary for elephants, Morgan would do whatever he could for them.

After dinner, the party moved to the kitchen. Max joined Leaf and Dan in helping Marian with the dishes. Clearly, the two men considered Max one of them, even though he had never washed a dish before. Because of him, the trio of Hetty's fathers was complete. He enjoyed the jovial comaraderie.

Hetty looked unusually tired, yet she appeared to delight in the harmony of her family. She rocked Pippa to sleep in her lap.

At the kitchen table, Katrinka brushed and braided Dora's hair. After a while she declared it was time to go home and get her beauty sleep.

She said, "Hetty honey, I won't need you to be at the lab tour tomorrow. It just complicates things when you're around." She winked at Max. "Hetty may be my lawyer, but I'm better in front of the camera."

Max kept his mouth shut. Hetty could deal with just about anything.

A Brightness of Hope

The ten days had passed too slowly in Morgan's absence, but he would be home from New York this afternoon. Hetty's impatience carried her through the forest and along a narrow path.

Many moments of importance had taken place in the presence of the magnificent oak tree, Hannah. It would happen again, today. Sweet memories and love for the old tree drove Hetty to quicken her pace. Throughout her lonely years of growing and adjusting, Hannah had been her friend and confidante.

Hannah would soon die, but thoughts of her would always be interwoven with Hetty's own joys and sorrows. Under Hannah's quiet majesty, she had discovered dear Leaf Locke was her father. And when Hetty was seventeen, and sick with love for Morgan, Hannah was the first to know.

The familiar path suddenly opened onto a strangely beautiful sight. Hannah dominated the clearing as she had in years past. Thick vines continued to weave and tangle their way up her massive trunk in a grand game of cat's cradle.

Once dependent on branches for support, the vines were now a lazy means of holding them in place. A single leaf floated to the forest floor, where partridgeberry and ivy matted the rich, dark soil. Several heavy branches lay rotting on the ground, apparently in harmony with some greater plan for their existence.

A chipmunk scurried from one to another, but stopped to watch the human intruder. A squirrel buried its acorn under the soft moss then flicked his tail, scolding Hetty for witnessing the hiding place. Hetty laughed aloud.

Acorns were early and plentiful. Why hadn't she noticed before? They were everywhere! Sprouts grew in the most amusing places. A crevice in the log had a cluster of new growth that might have started earlier in the spring.

Hannah's death would leave behind abundant new life.

Hetty pressed her hand against Hannah's rough bark. *Dear Hannah, I've come to say goodbye.* Hannah didn't need to say anything. The old tree seemed to understand. Love and gratitude had always been in this place.

A splash of sunlight led Hetty to a large flat rock. She needed to sit down. Spreading her skirt, she leaned back to savor this time and place. The rustle of leaves, the birdsongs—she could not take it all in, but listened with a pounding heart. A soft breeze lifted her hair, soft as the floss of a milkweed pod.

She closed her eyes and saw the dream more clearly: Morgan would take her hand. They would pass through the shadows. Rising together above the clouds, they would soar higher and higher . . . like eagles . . . up to the sun, with a perfect brightness of hope.

In silence, Morgan came from nowhere. First there was the fresh smell of his exertion—like rain on rolling hills or wind across the meadows. Then he was beside her, sharing her breath, rocking her in his arms; laughing at nothing and everything.

Wrapped in peace and contentment, Hetty was now complete. Only Hannah knew the secret thoughts that softened her eyes and glowed on her cheeks.

In his eagerness to see her, Morgan had not stopped at the cottage to shave. He flashed a smile in apology and brushed his knuckles against his jaw. It was a small gesture that made Hetty weak with love for him.

The deep blue of his eyes told of more to come. Her words could wait. She would keep still for his intentions to unfold.

Time stood still at his touch. Lost in time and space, they lay on a bed of soft green moss. A wood thrush blessed them with a song, until a hush fell over the forest. Hannah seemed to bow down, encircling them with a whisper of leaves.

The Perfect Day

The lacy green canopy above them shimmered with specks of golden sunlight. Awareness returned, and Hetty laughed with the chatter of a gray squirrel. Growing things stirred in the breeze, perfuming the air.

Morgan took her hand. Where was he taking her? No matter, they were together and would go from one joy to another. The path from the forest led to where their car was waiting.

Morgan drove along a narrow, winding road. The corners of his eyes crinkled as if a smile would soon appear. He had something in his pocket. It would keep. She would see soon enough.

At last the road fanned open to reveal a grand vista. Green fields stretched toward the crest of a hill. In the distance, a spot of white crouched behind a narrow band of trees.

It was the glider! A tow-plane was ready to launch it, and the pilot was talking with someone who looked like Ignatz. Was it?

Yes, and Freydis sat nearby in a chair. She held a parasol in one hand and waved to him with the other. Ignatz must have brought the chair from the cottage so Freydis could watch in comfort. Morgan took Hetty by the hand, and together they crossed the meadow to join them.

Freydis steadied herself between Ignatz and Hetty. After handshakes and greetings, Morgan's dark hair fell across his forehead, and he pulled a small box from his pocket. "For you, Ignatz," said Morgan.

"Like . . . like, you mean to open?"

Morgan nodded.

At first, Ignatz hesitated to open the deep blue velvet box. When he did, his enthusiasm exploded. "Man, oh man! You mean it? You get this offa some king or something?"

Morgan chuckled. "Freydis gave you a valuable watch," he said. "This should keep it safe. You want to see how to use it?"

It was a gold Albert chain with an enamel and gold watch fob on one end. Morgan demonstrated how to loop the chain through a vest buttonhole. Then he explained the watch fob.

"I had the jewelers make the Gorman family crest on one side," he said, "and Beverley on the other."

It was for Ignatz, but Hetty knew Morgan had also done it for her. When he turned to face her, the intense tenderness

Laughing at nothing and everything.

of Hetty's thoughts made her knees feel unsteady. He seemed to notice and supported her with an arm around her waist.

The gift for Ignatz represented what Hetty treasured most about Morgan—something she had hoped for. He had given trust to someone who needed it more than anyone they knew.

It was not only about Ignatz. There was also Morgan's kindness toward Max and his warm acceptance of Freydis in their home. These and other things bound her to him in a way nothing else could.

They soon settled into the cockpit of the glider, and Hetty nestled behind Morgan. The tow-plane launched them into a strong ridge lift. Beyond the crest of the hill, the blue expanse of heaven seemed to reach forever.

The towrope fell away, and they rose, circling from one thermal to another, feeling the lift under their wings—soaring with eagles high into the brilliance of the sun.

A vivid memory came to her. It was a dazzling performance in the circus ring. She was on the front row with her best friend Melinda Morganthal, when a magnificent man appeared in the spotlights. He glowed before them in a mask and a flowing cape. Hetty had been only twelve at the time, but she would never forget the way his dark hair fell across his forehead.

He threw back his cape and raised a tiny silver thimble in his white-gloved hand. The smallest corner of a red silk handkerchief peeked out from it. At first he barely pulled at the little corner, easing it out slowly. Then he pulled faster and faster, until suddenly, with a wondrous explosion of color, it seemed to engulf all space.

The glider rocked briefly. Hetty reached forward, tucking her fingers inside the neck of Morgan's shirt. Her touch was meant to convey trust, but she wondered if Morgan could feel the confusion of her emotions as well. If he should sense only the smallest corner of it peeking out, he would tug at

CHAPTER TEN 217

it—cautiously and slowly at first—until he could see both her joy and her fear. When the intensity of her turmoil could no longer be restrained, he would ease it out gently—then faster and faster—until it would explode in a billow of gray uncertainty.

But he would lift and pull her above the dreary mass, higher and higher, to soar on a cloud of white silk. Together they would float to a place clear and bright, in the pure brilliance of the sun. The perfect day was here and now.

Hetty was pale and lightheaded with anticipation. How had she planned to tell him? She couldn't remember, but she would do her best. Her fingertips lingered in his collar, cherishing the feel of his neck.

"Morgan, don't you think love matters more than anything?" she said. "Ideas come and go. People live and die. In the end, it's what we're left with that counts."

Her words kept tumbling out. "And I think the best thing of all—the thing that goes on forever is love. It's just that I love you so completely, there's no such thing as more," she said, "There's only longer. I mean having it go on longer. And hoping I can be everything you expect of me."

He laughed. "Just be more of the same. That's all I've ever wanted."

"Oh?" She was puzzled. "What does that mean?"

"It means follow your dreams," he said. "Wherever they go, I'm with you."

Hetty had waited so long to hear this from him. But his declaration was of little use now.

"Thank you," she said. "That means a lot to me." She hoped he couldn't detect the melancholy that tempered her gratitude.

Billowing clouds sifted the sunlight across hills and fields, allowing spots of brilliance to dance among the dark shadows. The pure white wings, the sacred silence of the sky, the unspoken miracles—they all expected reverence. As if awaiting words too sweet for even the most hushed utterance.

Leaning forward, Hetty pressed her face against the roughness of Morgan's cheek and whispered in his ear.

Stunned at her words, the color drained from his face. His jaw tightened, and his eyes seemed to lock on some nonexistent spot.

Slowly, they lost altitude. He circled the glider, spiraling down and down.

"Please be happy, Morgan!" she cried.

After what seemed an eternity of circling and dipping, he landed the glider gently in a field of tall grass then turned to her.

She trembled. "I wanted you to be happy," she said.

Morgan wasn't reacting as she had hoped. Darkness gripped her, and her turmoil was almost unbearable until she felt his embrace.

Then flooded with peace and contentment, she clung to her dearest dream. Morgan was everything good and true. If he should have to raise the children alone, they would know love.

"I lived through childbirth once," she said. "I could again."

Morgan held her against his shaking body and buried his face in her softness to hide the flow of tears.

THE END

Hetty on Hold is the fifth novel in the Hetty series by Martha Sears West. It follows *Hetty, Hetty Happens, Hetty or Not, and Honeymoon Summer.* West has also written and illustrated two children's books: *Longer than Forevermore,* and *Jake, Dad and the Worm.* Her book titled *Rhymes and Doodles from a Wind-up Toy* is a collection intended for all ages. All Martha's books have received the Mom's Choice© Award for excellence in family-friendly content.

COLOPHON

The Bembo Typeface

Bembo is a classic typeface that displays the characteristics that identify Old Style, humanist designs. It was drawn by Aldus Manutius and first used in 1496 for a 60-page text about a journey to Mount Aetna by a young humanist poet, Pietro Bembo, later a cardinal and secretary to Pope Leo X.

More recently, Bembo is the typeface used for volumes in the Everyman's Library series. Monotype Bembo is generally regarded as one of the most handsome revivals of Manutius' 15th century roman type.

The font size of the italic sections in *Hetty on Hold* is 12.5; otherwise, font size 12 has been used in the body of the text.

www.ingramcontent.com/pod-product-compliance
Lightning Source LLC
Chambersburg PA
CBHW031105080526
44587CB00011B/834